Changing Public and
Development Management:
South African Cases

LIBRARY
COPY

Changing Public and Development Management: South African Cases

(eds) Lauren Blythe Schütte
Erwin Schwella
Patrick FitzGerald

Juta & Co. Ltd

First published in 1995

© Juta & Co. Ltd.
P.O. Box 14373, Kenwyn 7790

This book is copyright under the Berne convention. In terms of the Copyright Act 98 of 1978, no part of this book may be reproduced or transmitted in any form or by any means (including photocopying, recording, or by any information storage and retrieval system) without permission in writing from the publisher.

ISBN 0 7021 3247 0

Subeditor: Angela Sayer-Farley, Cape Town
Book design and Desktop Publishing by Charlene Bate, Cape Town

Printed and bound in the Republic of South Africa by
Creda Press, Eliot Avenue, Epping II

CONTENTS

FOREWORD ix

PREFACE xi

LIST OF CONTRIBUTORS xiii

PART I:

AN INTRODUCTION TO CASE STUDIES 1
Lauren Blythe Schütte
THE USE OF CASE STUDIES IN PUBLIC AND DEVELOPMENT MANAGEMENT/
PUBLIC ADMINISTRATION 4
PRACTICAL HINTS FOR TEACHING CASES 5
   PREPARATION 5
   FACILITATION 6
CHOOSING A CASE 9
MAKING THE SHIFT 9

PART II: CASE STUDIES

1. **African Accountancy?**
   Patrick FitzGerald 12

2. **Mr Hoffman's Dilemma: Between a Rock and a Hard Place
   Recruitment in the Civil Service**
   Lauren Blythe Schütte 15

3. **Karl Smith, Adam Markswala and Pragmatism
   in Government Planning**
   Erwin Schwella 22

4. **A Principal, A Vision and Change in an
   Uncompromising Community, Part I**
   Sipho Sithole 30

5. **A Principal, A Vision and Change in an
   Uncompromising Community, Part II**
   Sipho Sithole 34

6. **Boomtown Déjà Vu**
   Fanie Cloete 38

7. **An Authoritarian Approach to Management**
   Salim Latib 45

8. **Johannesburg Hospital Nursing Services**
   Jacqui Myburgh 49

9. **Academic Management and Managing Academics**
   William Fox 69

10. **Careerists and Political Appointees in the Public Service: Conflicts in Policy Implementation**
    Msizi Fakude 74

11. **The Case of Zimetco**
    Merle Favis 77

12. **Going for Love, Money, Power, Politics or Principles**
    Fanie Cloete 81

13. **Molefe's Maze**
    Patrick Kelly 88

14. **Mikhukhu People of South Africa: A Question of Survival**
    Rams Ramashia 93

15. **Water, Water Everywhere and Not a Drop to Drink**
    Andries van Rooyen 97

16. **Putting Responsibility Where It Fits: A Question of Motivation at Tivumba Hospital**
    Lauren Blythe Schütte 101

17. **Bellrow Municipality Housing Department: An In-Basket Exercise**
    Erwin Schwella 105

18. **10111 – The Soweto Flying Squad**
    Jacqui Myburgh 112

19. **Spies That Came in from the Cold**
    Andries van Rooyen 122

20. **Policing in Rietspruit**
    Etienne Marais 132

21. **Life is Too Short to Drink Bad Wine: The Thorny Problem of Chardonnay that turned out to be Auxerrois**
    Erwin Schwella 136

22. **Towards a Policy on Hawking: A Role Play Exercise**
    Mark Swilling 142
23. **Thabiso Mabona and the Leeuwstroom Housing Department**
    Thabo Majoe and Lauren Blythe Schütte 148
24. **Affirmative Action in the Alexandra/Sandton Town Council**
    Haseena Rawat 152
25. **Management at the People's Development Centre:
    A Hard Nut to Crack**
    Mpho Moeti 155
26. **Peter Mahlangu and the Department of Works**
    Samson Baloyi 157
27. **Cracking the Culture Code: The Way into the Inner Circle**
    Joe Mokou 159
28. **Mountain Ridge Working Group:
    A New Response to Inner City Challenges**
    Lorelle Menné and Mark Bear 161

INDEX 166

FOREWORD

It is an honour to be asked to introduce the materials in this volume to the South African and international public – especially so because we know well how great an effort by how many is embodied here, and how much had to change for those persons to have even the chance to work together.

This groundbreaking first book of public and development management cases written by and for South Africans is the product of partnerships that themselves reflect the new South Africa. First was the partnership called the **New Public Administration Initiative,** which brought together individuals and faculties with distinct pasts willing to work jointly in forging the future. Second was the collaboration between that Initiative and an international partner of a sort from which South Africa had long been isolated.

It is just over three years ago that the NPAI and our own institution, the Kennedy School of Government at Harvard University, began to work together, thanks, most prominently, to the support of both a private corporation – the Otis Elevator company – and a non-profit institution, The Ford Foundation. Our initial goal was modest – to explore whether the diverse teaching methods and materials employed in teaching public officials in the United States might be of use in the new South Africa. These pedagogical approaches included the use of case studies, role playing and simulations, which, as a group, stood in contrast to what our South African colleagues called the logical-positivist "chalk-and-talk" style of instruction common in South African classrooms.

The initial effort involved forty South African and eight visitors from Harvard and Southern universities, who spent one week in January 1992 exploring the teaching and writing of case studies at the University of the Western Cape. The success of that initial workshop opened the door to further collaboration. Subsequent NPAI/Harvard annual workshops and case teaching and case writing have drawn participants from across the South African tertiary education landscape. The great majority of the South African faculties involved in teaching public and development administration have participated in these workshops. For those of us from outside South Africa, the experience has been challenging and rewarding.

In the introduction which follows, Lauren Blythe Schütte explains well the idea and practice of case teaching. Suffice to say here that we from the Kennedy School believed that we could help make a small contribution to the new South Africa through the development of a cadre of case teachers and a core of cases about public management. Cases, after all, have a lot to do with democracy. The development of cases – which are, after all, stories based on candid accounts – requires a government open enough to allow officials to share their experiences with those who write cases. The teaching of cases is predicated in open discussion, in which all points of view may be expressed.

Those of us involved in the Kennedy School's South Africa team – including Antonia Chayes, Herman "Dutch" Leonard, Kurt Campbell, John Thomas, Marty

Linsky, Linda Kaboolian, Ron David, Abe Chayes, Nancy Huntington and Gail Leftwich, as well as Leon Tarver and Damian Egigiri from Southern University – have our own memories of those moments when we realised that this collaboration, based on the idea of discussion-based learning, was really working.

But the proof that something important has truly taken place lies in the cases which follow. In them one can find narratives designed to help students confront and work through the toughest problems confronting South Africa – from affirmative action to township governance, from health care administration to police practice. It is our hope, and our expectation, that these stories will become familiar throughout South Africa; that, as happens at the Kennedy School, they will become points of reference for thoughtful people working on the problems of maintaining a vibrant public sector; that they will provoke discussions that will, ultimately, make for a new South Africa which is better managed, and therefore more prosperous and just, than it might otherwise have been. Cases, as stimulating as they are, are not ends in themselves. They are only the means to an improvement in practice.

In addition to the authors of the cases represented here, there are many others who have been involved in the NPAI-Kennedy School partnership. Their participation helped provide the forum in which these cases were tested and refined. We extend our own special thanks to all those who have participated in this collaboration and who are working to build the new South Africa.

Finally, a word about the editors. This book would not exist but for the vision and determination of its three editors: Patrick FitzGerald, one of the guiding spirits of the NPAI and the founding director of the WITS P&DM programme; Erwin Schwella, also a founder of NPAI and long a pillar and leader in South African public administration; and Lauren Schütte, a person of great skill and craft who is leading the first case-writing programme in South Africa.

You hold in your hand a book which represents a first step toward the development of a new form of training for the public administration in South Africa. It's our hope that it will prove both useful and inspiring, and that this volume will be the first of many.

Peter Zimmerman
Associate Dean for Teaching Programs
Kennedy School of Government
Harvard University

Howard Husock
Director: Case Program
Kennedy School of Government
Harvard University

June, 1994
Cambridge, MA

PREFACE

The fires of change have swept through South Africa, as they have throughout the world, rendering old ways of doing things and old organisational forms, structures and processes inappropriate.

The development challenges facing us require accountable and effective public managers who are able to lead and redesign organisations for strategic development tasks. Development challenges have thus increasingly become human resource challenges, and the debates around the major task of capacity building, are now focused in a national reconstruction and development programme. This South African Reconstruction and Development Programme (RDP) defines human resource development as a "process in which the citizens of a nation acquire and develop the knowledge and skill necessary for occupational tasks and for other social, cultural, intellectual and political roles that are part and parcel of a vibrant democratic society". For the RDP to be realised, the South African public service requires well trained persons with a proactive, problem-solving orientation and attitude. People who are capable of analysing, reflecting, deciding and, most importantly, acting appropriately. Universities and technikons need to guarantee that their public management graduates go out into this new world equipped with skills to improve organisational performance for the development goals of the society.

Current South African thinking in the public administration field is in that our theory and practice is undergoing a paradigm shift *away* from the logical-positivist world view which had until recently gone unchallenged, *towards* a more value oriented and contextual approach. During the past few years, public administration academics gathered under the umbrella of the *New Public Administration Initiative* have declared the traditional mode of teaching public administration in South Africa, which stressed out-dated generic administrative processes and utilised exclusively "chalk-and-talk" teaching methods, wholly redundant in the post-apartheid reality. This significant change in our operating paradigm is occurring within the broader context of a global shift towards a post-modern world where different thinking tracks criss-cross or run in parallel or diverge in complex patterns.

This new intellectual environment should be understood in the context of the scientific paradigm shift which began at the turn of the century when discoveries in physics revealed a whole new sub-atomic world made up of nothing more than energy – a world of uncertainty where truth could no longer be objectively verified. Light, it was discovered, could equally be proven to be wave-like as it could be particle-like and only the choice of experiment made by the individual determined the result. In simple terms, this paradigm change displaces the human senses as the central test of reality and elevates human inner wisdom and authority, as well as lived experience to centre stage.

Transformations in our knowledge framework have profound effects on every aspect of our daily lives. The shift that we are currently undergoing has important implications for our conception of teaching and learning. Those who have come through an educational system in which the "banking" or "teacher-tell" concept of education is employed, in which knowledge is "bestowed" from teacher to student, have little practice in bringing their own inner wisdom and subjective authority to bear in decision making. Nor, for that matter, in trusting their own judgements, perceptions and interpretations of reality as they wait patiently for the "expert" to interpret reality and pass down proclamations.

If public administration theory and practice in South Africa is to truly achieve a new development-friendly paradigm, then the need for fresh teaching methodologies takes on central importance. Discussion-based teaching, utilising tools such as case studies, provides students with the opportunity to practice tapping into their own life experience in order to interpret reality and decide on appropriate action; to observe, analyse, select, decide and act. Because case studies appear as autonomous entities, and are not accompanied by analysis, students need to be able to draw on their own experiential knowledge in order to interpret the situation in the case study and to determine action. In addition, case studies develop students' ability to make linkages between practice and theory, thus enhancing their ability to apply their learning to work, career and life contexts.

The pace of change witnessed in the world in general, and South Africa in particular, implies that organisations, both public and private, will have to become what Senge calls "Learning Organisations", constantly enhancing their capacity to create. In a post-modern world, more flexible structures and modes of inter-institutional co-operation will have to be adopted in order to cope with turbulent organisational and environmental conditions. As boundaries become less clear, vision and mission become all-important, thus giving dialogue a central role in the organisation. The use of case studies in the training of managers provides students with the practice needed to be able to play a meaningful role in the conversations of the organisations in which they find employment, in vocalising the vision and determining the mission.

A start has been made in the implementation of discussion-based teaching in public administration departments in South Africa. For this achievement, acknowledgement and thanks go to the team from the Kennedy School of Government who have visited this country over the past few years in order to build capacity in the areas of case teaching and case writing.

This book is a compilation of local cases written by South Africans, gathered together in the hope that they will encourage more wide-spread use of case teaching in public administration classrooms in order that we may experience this much touted paradigm shift. Take them and use them and create others for further publications. There are many stories to be told and many students with whom to teach and learn.

The Editors
Lauren Blythe Schütte
Erwin Schwella
Patrick FitzGerald

LIST OF CONTRIBUTORS

Samson Baloyi is the Chief Quantity Surveyor for the Gazankulu Government. He holds a BSc as well as a PDM(PPDA) from the Graduate School of Public and Development Management at the University of the Witwatersrand (GSP&DM (Wits)).

G S (Fanie) Cloete is Professor of Public and Development Management at the School of Public Management at the University of Stellenbosch. He holds an LLB degree (RAU) as well as an MA and PhD in Political Science from the University of Stellenbosch.

Merle Favis is the Senior Programme Officer at Interfund. She holds a BA(Hons) as well as a PDM(PPDA) from the GSP&DM (Wits).

Msizi Fakude is a teacher at Pace Community College. He holds a BA(Hons) as well as a PDM(PPDA) from the GSP&DM (Wits).

Patrick FitzGerald is the Director of the Graduate School of Public & Development Management at the University of the Witwatersrand. He holds an MPA from the University of Liverpool.

William Fox is an Associate Professor in Public and Development Management at the School of Public Management at the University of Stellenbosch. He holds the degrees of BA(Hons) (Unisa) MA (Natal) and PhD from the University of Stellenbosch.

Patrick Kelly is the National Director of the Human Rights Commission. He holds a BA(Hons) as well as a PDM(PPDA) from the GSP&DM (Wits).

Salim Latib is a lecturer at the Graduate School of Public and Development Management at the University of the Witwatersrand. He holds a B Admin (UDW) and a Politics Honours (Wits) as well as a PDM(PPDA) from the GSP&DM (Wits).

Etienne Marais is a lecturer and Convenor of the Police Management Programme, Graduate School of Public & Development Management at the University of the Witwatersrand. He holds a BA as well as an Honours degree from the same university.

Thabo Majoe is currently the Director of the North West Region National Literacy Corporation. He holds a BA in Sociology and Politics as well as a PDM(PPDA) from the GSP&DM (Wits).

Lorelle Menné MA Ind Psych (UN) MBA (UCT) and Mark Bear MA (Cambridge) MBA (UCT) are both business consultants.

Mpho Moeti is a management trainee at Boumat and holds a BA in Industrial Sociology and Political Studies (Wits) as well as a PDM(PPDA) from the GSP&DM (Wits).

Joe Mokou is an administrative assistant with the United Nations High Commission for Refugees. He holds a BA from the University of the North as well as a PDM(PPDA) from the GSP&DM (Wits).

Jacqui Myburgh is reading for her doctorate at Cambridge University. She was previously the case writer at the Wits Business School.

Rams Ramashia is an associate director at Private Agencies Collaborating Together (PACT).

Haseena Rawat is a partner in Training and Development Options. She holds a BA MEd and a PDM(PPDA) from the GSP&DM (Wits).

Lauren Schütte is a lecturer as well as the Case Study Co-ordinator at the Graduate School of Public and Development Management at the University of the Witwatersrand. She holds a BA(Hons) from the University of Natal, Durban as well as a PDM(PPDA) from the GSP&DM (Wits).

Erwin Schwella is the Director: School of Public Management at the University of Stellenbosch. He holds the degrees BA (Law) BA Honours (Sociology) Honours in Public Administration MPA and PhD (P&DM).

Sipho Sithole is the Human Resource Manager of Airports Company Ltd. He has an MSc Industrial Relations and Personnel Management from the London School of Economics and Political Science, University of London.

Mark Swilling is a senior lecturer at the Graduate School of Public and Development Management at the University of the Witwatersrand. He holds a BA(Hons) in Politics from that university and a PhD from the University of Warwick.

Andries van Rooyen is a senior lecturer in the School of Public Management at the University of Stellenbosch. He studied for his B Admin Honours B Admin and M Admin at the same university.

PART ONE

AN INTRODUCTION TO CASE STUDIES

AN INTRODUCTION TO CASE STUDIES

by Lauren Blythe Schütte

Perhaps the best way to explain what a case is is to describe what it is not. A case study is not just a good story although it could be described as a management, policy or organisational situation presented in story form. Case studies approximate management and policy activities by presenting, usually in narrative form, but also in the form of newspaper articles, photographs or video-clips, a particular problem or difficulty faced by an individual or organisation which requires resolution; a situation which requires action or an ethical dilemma which requires deliberation. What really makes a case a case is that it is not a story written for entertainment purposes alone but is designed to achieve specific learning objectives, requiring independent, critical, problem-solving thinking patterns on the part of the students.

Cases require that students identify and analyse problems, form reasoned, defensible interpretations and reach and test conclusions unaided (Wilkinson & Dubrow, 1991: 249). Through cases, therefore, learning occurs on two levels: students learn about the subject matter of the case at the same time as they master process skills. Because there is never one solution to a problem, cases provide an excellent opportunity for students to develop independent thinking patterns and to lessen their propensity to defer to lecturers' "expert" points of view.

Cases represent a break with traditional, conventional lecture and textbook instruction which sets the instructor or lecturer up as an expert prescribing answers to a group of avid disciples. They represent instead an extensively utilised tool in discussion pedagogy where interactive, experiential learning is encouraged. In Teacher-Tell methodology, the lecturer remains in control of the classroom, confident that, as the expert in a topic, she will be able to deliver to her students, in a highly structured manner, a considerable body of facts in which they will be able to demonstrate proficiency come the exams. There is little emphasis on critical thinking or active engagement on the part of the students in this type of classroom. Interactive discussion, on the other hand, encourages self-discovery amongst students. There is shared responsibility for the learning process. The lecturer is no longer solely responsible for delivering expert knowledge but for provoking healthy discussion in order to develop critical thinking amongst students.

Cases then, are designed not simply to entertain, nor merely to provide students with knowledge on a particular topic, but also to provide training in independent thinking, rigorous analysis and problem solving. The case-study method was developed to approximate the way people derive their information and make decisions in life (Meyer & Brown, 1989: 7). Cases are therefore ideal tools for management education as they introduce students to a variety of experiences in a short space of time in a relatively safe environment, allowing students to experiment with various solutions and actions without serious consequences. They provide students with the opportunity to learn not only from their own active participation but from the contributions of others. Case studies provide students with opportunities to question their own assumptions and broaden their points of view. They may have to identify with characters in the case studies with whom they may have no empathy, forcing them to look at the situation presented in the case from all angles and perspectives.

David Garvin, in his essay "Barriers and Gateways to Learning" (1991: 10), outlines the need for three fundamental shifts for the successful practice of discussion teaching and other forms of active learning:

- A shift in the *balance of power* in the classroom away from a situation where the lecturer is all-powerful to a more democratic environment where students feel comfortable sharing in the discussion and decision making;
- A shift in the *locus of attention* away from a singular concern for the material to an equal focus on content, the classroom process and the learning climate;
- A shift in *instructional skills* away from declarative explanations to questioning, listening and responding.

Discussion teaching, and the use of case studies, obviously requires more involvement and commitment on the part of the lecturer as well as on the part of the students than traditional chalk-and-talk teaching, as it entails helping students find their own way to material rather than bringing the material to the student (Christensen, 1991: 24). The role of the lecturer in this methodology shifts dramatically away from the expert telling, to one of facilitating learning and encouraging discussion (Garvin, 1991: 11). Lecturers no longer have to be responsible for the content alone but also for the learning process. This requires that lecturers not only have knowledge of their particular topic but also good interpersonal skills and awareness of group dynamics.

Through discussion teaching, students become active participants in the learning process rather than passive recipients. This puts the students under certain obligations which are absent in traditional classroom situations. Successful participative learning requires that students have a personal investment in the learning process. Students need a sense of "ownership" of the learning process in order to feel free enough to participate in discussions. This sense of "ownership" can be encouraged by the creation of a supportive environment in the classroom.

Vital to the success of case teaching, and indeed the use of other tools in interactive teaching, are good facilitation skills. Mastery of these skills may seem difficult for lecturers who are schooled in the Teacher-Tell method but with some practice it can be done. Shifting to this methodology will bring its rewards through enhanced vigour in the classroom and greater confidence amongst your students.

THE USE OF CASE STUDIES IN PUBLIC AND DEVELOPMENT MANAGEMENT/ PUBLIC ADMINISTRATION

The process of political transition in South Africa will, of necessity, be accompanied by a process of administrative reform. The role of the civil service in post-apartheid South Africa is more appropriately that of servant of the public and provider of services, than that of an instrument of state power and controller of the public. The public service will be required to play a vital role in the delivery of services to all South Africans and will have to become more client-centred. In addition, the enormity of the challenges facing the new government will mean that the public service will be called upon to participate more directly in policy formulation and decision making, which will require greater consultation with clients and other stake-holders, both in developing proposals and in administering programmes. The discipline of Public Administration in South Africa has recognised the need to adapt its training to fit the requirements of this new responsive civil service and is, indeed, undergoing a fundamental shift in paradigm (see FitzGerald, 1993).

On 26 November 1991 the Mount Grace Resolution was adopted by a band of public and development management *aficionados* in the Magaliesburg (Fitz-Gerald, 1993: 4). The adoption of the resolution gave shape and form to the emerging movement within the South African discipline already at the time known as the **New Public Administration Initiative (NPAI)**. The resolution declared the existing theory, practice and paradigm of existing public administration in South Africa wholly redundant and that:

"New approaches to the study, teaching and practice of Public Administration are necessary. These should entail:
- an explicit normative focus on, *inter alia:*
  - promoting more democratic, inclusive and participatory government and public service at all levels of government;
  - a just, equitable and non-racial society with equal access for all people to societal resources;
  - providing better public services to people to enable them to improve their quality of life and become more self-reliant;
  - maintaining suitable economic, social and political growth and development; and
  - promoting values such as efficiency, effectiveness, productivity, accountability, responsibility and responsiveness.
- more rigorous scientific analysis, explanation and prediction of governmental phenomena supplementing their mere description is necessary.
- an open and critical debate on explanatory models for this purpose must be encouraged.
- an explicit developmental focus instead of a control and regulation oriented one must be established. This could include rationalisation between Public Administration and Development Administration.

- developing proactive and useful international networks.

In this way, a more relevant approach to governmental issues in a developing society will be achieved" (McLennan & FitzGerald, 1992: 23).

These resolutions represent a strong argument for the development of new teaching methodologies which will replace the old administrative paradigm which is procedure and control oriented (McLennan, 1993). The new paradigm, which is fast becoming conventional wisdom, will require methodologies that will provide students with a more proactive, developmental ethos; methodologies that will turn the current catchwords – efficiency, effectiveness, public participation, accountability, responsiveness, equity and empowerment – into real concepts for students of public and development management.

Case studies, and other interactive methodologies, will do more to prepare future administrators for the problems and challenges left behind by the apartheid legacy than traditional, prescriptive, academic study. Before they leave the sanctuary of the classroom, students will have been faced with real ethical dilemmas, they will have solved organisational problems, restructured departments, drawn up policy proposals, strategised about staff motivation and faced a myriad other management and policy situations. They will have developed the ability to make decisions based on the facts before them as well as to adapt decisions to changing circumstances.

What is needed to make widespread use of case studies in South African public administration institutions possible, is a bank of local case studies. Whilst international experiences are informative and necessary, students also need local cases to which they can easily relate to ensure that maximum learning takes place. Language and scenarios should be familiar and situations conceivable in order for students to be able to actively engage with the case study.

PRACTICAL HINTS FOR TEACHING CASES

The success of the case study method depends largely on the level of discussion and debate in the classroom (Meyer, 1989: 7). High-level debate requires that both participants and discussion leaders are well prepared.

Preparation

Students should come to class having read the case thoroughly and having identified the major issues in the case as well as the motivations of the people involved. Analysis and discussion of cases is a self-learning process, the benefits of which are maximised through rigorous debate, and it is therefore of utmost importance that participation in the discussion is high.

High-level participation can be encouraged by discussion leaders through the development of a learning contract within the classroom. A contract can encourage the development of what Christensen calls a "Learning Community" (1991: 19) which holds in high regard values such as civility, willingness to take risks and appreciation of diversity. Mutual respect amongst participants and between participants and discussion leader is imperative as a confrontational atmosphere in the classroom is sure to drive out discussion, particularly from those who may feel themselves to be less articulate. Students should feel free to defend their positions but without dogmatism, as there is seldom only one answer to a dilemma or one solution to a problem. Debate and cross-questioning should occur in an assertive, yet respectful and civil environment to be of any benefit (Meyer, 1989: 8). A contract with students can promote deep commitment, encourage accountability and mutual responsibility and build a sense of collegiality within the class.

Discussion leaders need to be even more prepared than the students. Not only do they have to be minutely familiar with the case but they should be able to anticipate the many responses which the students will have to the case. The discussion leader needs to be very clear what she wants to achieve out of the case discussion so she can steer the discussion in the right direction.

Facilitation

Good facilitation of case studies requires mastery of skills in questioning, listening and response. Discussion leaders can direct the debate in the right direction by asking the right questions. Development of competency in questioning is an intuitive process which can be refined only through experience. Christensen has suggested that in order to successfully elicit participation in the class, discussion leaders should develop an extensive repertoire of questions. He has developed a typology of questions (1991: 158) which are useful but by no means exhaustive. They include **open-ended questions** asking for general reactions to the case; **diagnostic questions**, asking for analysis of the problem in the case; **information-seeking questions**, asking for specific details; **challenging or testing questions**, forcing students to question their beliefs or arguments; **action questions**, requesting students to outline a plan of action; **prediction questions**, asking students to forecast consequences of solutions; **hypothetical questions**, asking students to think about possible outcomes of alternative actions, and **questions of generalisation**, asking students to step outside of the case to look at the broader themes raised in the case.

Listening skills are vitally important for good class discussion and need to be cultivated not only in the discussion leader but also in discussion participants. Good listening is not a passive activity but requires intense concentration as it is not merely about hearing but also about synthesising facial expressions, gestures and so on (Leonard, 1991: 138) in order to really get to the meaning of the communication. Discussion leaders need to listen to and assess a student's contribution on two levels: firstly for content and secondly, and perhaps more importantly, for continuity and value to the discussion. A good listener is able to build on the ideas of previous contributors, and students should be encouraged to respond to the previous speaker before moving the discussion in another direction. Class discussion can be stymied by poor listening skills on the part of both students and

discussion leaders. Leonard has identified a number of listening pathologies (1991: 140-145), such as:
- **The Mortar Lob:** When a student has prepared one single contribution to the discussion and spends the entire session trying to decide when the cue has been given to "lob" the "mortar" into the discussion. When the student thinks that the cue has arrived, the mortar is fired often without due regard for building on the previous speaker's comment. Discussion leaders, Leonard suggests, can deal with this pathology by encouraging students to provide a link between the new observation and the preceding discussion;
- **The Pit Bull:** When students within the group slip into a pattern of relentlessly pursuing one particular issue from one perspective only. When this happens, the pit bull listens only for the right opening to pursue his or her hobby horse and the rest of the class tunes out and stops listening. Leonard suggests that the remedy for this is to require the pit bull to present different points of view.

Discussion leaders are by no means exempt from listening pathologies, a few of which Leonard calls:
- **The Teacher's Express:** When a programme is billed as a discussion but is really a lecture, with the instructor "driving the class through a preordained discussion". In this scenario, the instructor does not listen to contributions carefully and students are inclined to feel that they are there to fill in the gaps rather than to think creatively;
- **Hiding the Ball:** When the instructor has in mind a preferred answer to a question and is waiting for this response before moving on to the next item in a preordained agenda. Students feel that they are being asked to play a guessing game and discussion becomes sterile;
- **Everything Goes:** When instructor and class "operate in the mode of false affirmation" out of an attempt to make members of the group feel safe and at ease. In this pathology, every comment is treated as though it were profound and appropriate, which can lead to the discussion degenerating into what Leonard describes as "a dying fish flapping on the docks".

Perhaps the most difficult of the three skills necessary for good facilitation is the art of responding to students' contributions. Response is the "art of the immediate". It is impossible to prepare a reponse in advance and yet responses have the most impact on the nature of the discussion (Christensen, 1991: 166). Appropriate responses depend very much on the lecturer's ability to read the mood of the group and to predict what effect certain responses will have on the individual and the group as a whole. The most important skill to acquire is to know how to challenge students without undermining their contributions. Often allowing an unhelpful or inappropriate response to hang in the air without reply can be very damaging to the self-esteem of the student. The challenge is to find constructive ways of forcing the student to think more rigorously about issues. This can be achieved by allowing the student another chance to reformulate his position or to raise further questions on the issue.

Students who are used to traditional teaching methodologies will need to be encouraged to have a point of view and to express original thought. Students who are wary of participation should receive support and encouragement from the discussion leader even when making a point that is not particularly brilliant, although the need for sensitivity should be weighed against the need for students to learn to deal with criticism. "The ability to survive public criticism, after all, is an important professional skill, and one that must be learned" (Garvin, 1991: 296). It is surely better to learn this skill in a supportive environment than in a committee room. Public praise, however, can be as damaging to the learning process as public blame, as it reinforces the stereotype that there is only one right answer (Christensen, 1991: 170).

In order to be fair to the discussion process and to the class, discussion leaders need to be able to bring students who are going off at a tangent back to the main discussion without making them feel that their contributions were totally meaningless. The ability to balance fairness to the discussion process with fairness to the feelings of the individual student is a delicate act which depends very much on the intuition and sensitivity of the discussion leader. It is tempting to call on students who we know will move the discussion into deeper territory and to ignore those we feel may not contribute much, but it is important to be fair to all students in order to maintain that Learning Community mentioned earlier. Lecturers may be guided in this by Garvin's distinction that fair treatment does not necessarily mean standardised treatment, as students clearly have different needs. Different and appropriate treatment does not mean that different standards are being applied; it simply means that individuals are being treated in ways that acknowledge their differences as individuals and are being offered "equal opportunities to excel" (Garvin, 1991: 290).

Only the individual discussion leader will really know how to handle this delicate balancing act but this requires that they get to know their students better than is necessary in traditional classrooms. This is not to say that the lecturer need know personal details about the students' lives but rather that they be aware of dynamics between students and sensitive to individual levels of confidence.

Just as there is no single answer to a case, there is no one correct way of studying a case. The choice of approach will depend on the complexity of the case as well as on the size of the class. Regardless of the method chosen, study of a case should always start with independent, personal study of the material to ensure that each student is familiar with the issues.

As part of their preparation, students may be asked to apply their minds to specific questions outlined at the end of the case or simply to try and identify the major issues raised by the material. Individual preparation is an important and essential basis for wider class discussion.

It is often useful in larger classes or when discussing more complex cases to divide the class into smaller groups to discuss the case after individual preparation and before wider class discussion. This technique serves to give each student, particularly those who may feel reluctant to participate in large groups, the opportunity to partake in the discussion. These smaller groups may be asked to address particular topics or themes present in the case for subsequent participation in wider class discussion or for formal presentation. This technique may serve to tighten up the discussion when there are a large number of participants or when the case is complex and multi-faceted.

CHOOSING A CASE

Selecting an existing case for use in the classroom or deciding on which lead to follow when developing a new case is a tricky process particularly for lecturers new to the case teaching methodology. Dorothy Robyn, Assistant Professor of Public Policy at the Kennedy School, provides some assistance by identifying five criteria which capture the essence of what makes a good case (1986). First, she argues, a case should have **pedagogic utility**. It should be able to serve a particular teaching function by raising particular pedagogic issues. A good rule of thumb when choosing a case, she argues, is that every case needs a theory and should be thought of, not in isolation, but as an integral part of a module.

Secondly, a good case should be **conflict provoking**, as controversy stimulates good case discussion and forces students to think through their decisions thoroughly whilst demonstrating that there are generally no right answers.

Thirdly, Robyn points out that a good case is **decision forcing**, or open ended. Such a case presents a choice or decisions confronting a manager or analyst, without revealing what the protagonist did or the consequences of that action. Open-ended cases encourage greater engagement than do retrospective cases.

The fourth characteristic of a good case is its **generality**, its ability to illustrate general lessons related to some larger class of managerial or analytic problem. The environmental tenet "Think Globally, Act Locally" is a useful analogy to reinforce this point: a good case can be described as one which stimulates discussion on broad, "global" issues whilst forcing action or decision on a more specific "local" situation.

Brevity, the final characteristic of a good case, is also essential, Robyn argues, to allow discussion to evolve to higher levels of abstraction. Overly long and complex cases often impede this process by bogging students down in irrelevant facts.

MAKING THE SHIFT

Mastering the art of discussion pedagogy and the use of case studies may seem an impossible task for some but, be assured, it can be accomplished through practice and experimentation and the rewards certainly justify the effort involved. It may be difficult for lecturers to come to terms with their new, less obtrusive, role in the classroom, but they still have an important role to play, perhaps even more so, in the creation of a learning community within the classroom. Their guidance and facilitation are crucial in ensuring that the classroom becomes a veritable engine room of discussion and discovery.

Lecturers' efforts will be rewarded with the knowledge that their students will go out into the working world, confident and able to deal with the many ambiguous situations they will face in their working lives as public managers.

REFERENCES

Christensen, C R; Garvin, D A & Sweet A (eds.) 1991. *Education for Judgement. The Artistry of Discussion Leadership*, Boston: Harvard Business School Press

Christensen, C R. 'Premises and Practices of Discussion Teaching'; in Christensen, C R; Garvin, D A & Sweet A (eds.) 1991. *Education for Judgement. The Artistry of Discussion Leadership*, Boston: Harvard Business School Press

Christensen, C R. 'Every Student Teaches and Every Teacher Learns: The Reciprocal Gift of Discussion Teaching', in Christensen, C R; Garvin, D A & Sweet A (eds.) 1991. *Education for Judgement. The Artistry of Discussion Leadership*, Boston: Harvard Business School Press

Christensen, C R. 'The Discussion Teacher in Action: Questioning, Listening and Response', in Christensen, C R; Garvin, D A & Sweet A (eds.) 1991. *Education for Judgement. The Artistry of Discussion Leadership*, Boston: Harvard Business School Press

FitzGerald, P. *An Emerging Paradigm in South African Public and Development Management*: Paper presented at the Fourth Winelands Conference: Public and Development Management for Africa: 29 Sep – 1 Oct 1993, Stellenbosch, South Africa

Garvin, D A. 'Barriers and Gateways to Learning', in Christensen, C R; Garvin, D A & Sweet A (eds.) 1991. *Education for Judgement. The Artistry of Discussion Leadership*, Boston: Harvard Business School Press

Garvin, D A. 'A Delicate Balance: Ethical Dilemmas and the Discussion Process', in Christensen, C R; Garvin, D A & Sweet A (eds.) 1991. *Education for Judgement. The Artistry of Discussion Leadership*, Boston: Harvard Business School Press

Hansen, A J. 'Establishing a Teaching/Learning Contract', in Christensen, C R; Garvin, D A & Sweet A (eds.) 1991. *Education for Judgement. The Artistry of Discussion Leadership*, Boston: Harvard Business School Press

Leonard, H B. 'With Open Ears: Listening and the Art of Discussion Leading', in Christensen, C R; Garvin, D A & Sweet A (eds.) 1991. *Education for Judgement. The Artistry of Discussion Leadership*, Boston: Harvard Business School Press

McLennan, A. 'The Toyi-toyiing Civil Servant' in Van Zyl Slabbert (ed.) 1993. *Restructuring the State*, DSA In Depth – Aug-Sep

McLennan, A & FitzGerald, P. 1991. *The Mount Grace Papers*, Johannesburg: Public and Development Management Programme

Pastoll, G. 1992. *Tutorials That Work, A Guide to Running Effective Tutorials*. Cape Town: Arrow Publishers

Robyn, D. 1986. *What Makes A Good Case*, Kennedy School of Government Case Program, Unpublished Paper

Thandi, H S & Rafaei, S M K W. 1989. *Case Writing: A Guide*, Malaysia: Pelanduk Publications

Wilkinson, J & Dubrow, H. 'Encouraging Independent Thinking', in Christensen, C R; Garvin, D A & Sweet A (eds.) 1991. *Education for Judgement. The Artistry of Discussion Leadership*, Boston: Harvard Business School Press

PART TWO

CASE STUDIES

CASE STUDY ONE

AFRICAN ACCOUNTANCY?

Patrick FitzGerald

Excerpt from "From African Accountancy – Ancient and Modern" by Robert Lacville, *Guardian Weekly*, 23–29 October 1992

The African Princess picked up her first job as administrator (or business manager) in an engineering consultancy. She had returned from Europe to her country (which is somewhere in Africa) with a management degree, and was keen to launch herself into a professional career. Her employer, Mr Koita, had started his consultancy with a portfolio of projects mainly from the European Community, and mostly in agriculture: drainage systems, irrigation plants, small barrages, and suchlike useful pieces of agricultural infrastructure. It was a good job for a young manager, and the Princess arrived on that first Monday morning full of enthusiasm and encouragement.

Her boss called her into his office. He dumped his briefcase on the desk, and told the Princess that since the previous Administrator had left three weeks previously, none of the office bills had been paid. She should get the accumulated bills from his secretary, and make sure the company didn't lose its telephone, electricity, and other supplies because of unpaid bills! Then he opened the briefcase, and turned out a few dozen packages of bank notes. Mr Koita had just been to the bank.

The Princess sat down expectantly, ready to count the bank notes. Mr Koita picked up two packages, and put one in each pocket. "You can take the rest to your office to count them," he said; "I have a meeting at 10am." The amazed Princess picked up the bank notes and staggered back to her office to count them. She collected the bills from the secretary, and spent the next two days phoning suppliers, paying bills, and entering the accounts. There was no strong box, so she had to take all the spare money back home with her, she didn't dare leave it in the office overnight. People must have wondered why she was hugging her bag to her stomach all week!

The following Monday, Mr Koita called her up. "How much money do you need this week?" he asked. "Well, I can't tell how much we shall spend," she replied, "but there is still $400 left from last week." "Oh well, that's O.K. then," said Koita. He dismissed her with a wave. She went back into her office, sank her head into her hands, and wondered what to do. "This week there is $400 left over, and he is surprised," she thought, "but next time it might be the other way around! Suppose he thinks there is $400 left over, when in fact all the money has gone to pay the bills?" The Princess felt uneasy. But she completed her day's accounts and went home with her uncomfortable bag of money.

On the Tuesday, Mr Koita asked the Administrator to go and buy some duplicating paper: ten reams for a series of reports which would be ready the next day. The Princess drove off in the company car, and the driver took her to see the usual supplier. She checked the prices against the previous invoices, approved the purchase, loaded up the ten reams of paper, and asked for the invoice. The invoice was correct. The Princess dipped into her bag, pulled out the money, and paid. The receipt was given, and the Princess packed up her bag again and went off towards the door.

"Madame," called the shop manager, "your 10% discount". The Princess looked back. There was a bundle of bank-notes being held across the counter. She counted the notes. Sure enough, 10%. So she thanked the man, and drove back to the office. But on her accounts, she got stuck. Where would she put the 10% discount? If she accounted it as reduced cost, the invoice would differ from the amount in the ledger. Should she put it in as income? That didn't seem right either. Remember this was the Princess's first job, so she went round next door to ask a colleague what they usually did with the discounts. The colleague grinned: "The discount is for you." In those days the Princess was still very innocent. She asked again how to explain the discount. "Keep it, girl!" said the colleague. "If you don't want it, you can give it to me and I'll chop it plenty fast!"

The Princess didn't put it into her purse. She went to her office, sank her head into her hands, and had a long think. Once she decided what to do, she sat up straight, and carefully divided the money into three parts. She gave one part to the office cleaner, one to the driver, and one to the leper sitting outside the front door. Then she took out a piece of writing paper and wrote: "Dear Mr Koita, I am afraid that I cannot work correctly in your organisation, where the rules are not conducive to an honest accounting system. Please find enclosed my accounts and the $320 remaining from the money you gave me last Monday. Yours sincerely ..."

"There is nothing criminally wrong with Mr Koita's system," she told me. "It is, after all, his consultancy, it is his money, and he is entitled to do what he likes with it. But it is African management, not professional management, and it leads to misunderstandings. And because there are no controls, it leads often to corruption. I didn't want to work there: I preferred to be unemployed. And I was for three months until I joined another consulting firm."

DISCUSSION QUESTIONS

1. Comment on the implicit ethos at work in Mr Koita's engineering consultancy.
2. What is the problem as the African Princess sees it? Do you agree with the distinction she makes between different styles of management?
3. What, if anything, should be done to instill an ethos of professional management into the consultancy?

4. What political/social/ethical/cultural/environmental changes would assist with the effectiveness of any suggested remedies?
5. If you had found yourself in this situation would you have reacted differently? If so, how would you have responded?

CASE STUDY TWO

MR HOFFMAN'S DILEMMA: BETWEEN A ROCK AND A HARD PLACE: RECRUITMENT IN THE CIVIL SERVICE

Lauren Blythe Schütte

A TROUBLING PHONE CALL

A tall, greying man bent over the big mahogany desk. He let go of the small silver ball he held between his thumb and index finger and watched it swing into the row of silver balls hanging off the frame of his executive toy. His eyes flicked backwards and forwards watching the rhythm he had set in motion, while the clicking sounds calmed his anxious thoughts. The shrill sound of his telephone ringing broke his troubled reverie. "Hoffman!" he barked into the receiver. After a few minutes, he put down the receiver and sighed. Yet another problem to deal with! He had told his secretary to screen all his calls; he didn't have the time to handle problems like this!

The phone call was from a young woman, Vicky Ramarumo, who claimed that in February she had been offered a position over the telephone, as a Senior Planner in the Directorate of Development Planning but was still awaiting a formal letter of appointment. It was now July! Mr Hoffman wondered what could be going on. This was not the only phone call of this nature he had received. He cast his mind back over the activities of the past few months in an attempt to analyse the situation.

BACKGROUND INFORMATION

Mr Hoffman is the Director of Office Administration in a large government department and is responsible for personnel provision and utilisation within the department. His responsibilities include the administration of staff affairs and the utilisation of each officer and employee to the greatest benefit of the department. He operates alongside a number of other Directors under the umbrella of the Chief Directorate for Administrative Support, headed by Mr Van Zyl. His colleagues head up the following directorates:

Directorate: Efficiency, which renders a management advisory service to the Department and is directed towards the improvement of efficiency and effectiveness of the organisation;

Directorate: Information Services, which is responsible for the dissemination of relevant information to management officials within its and other government departments as well as to key role-players in the field of development;

Directorate: Communication Services, which provides a liaison service between the department and the public and media, as well as publication, audio visual and graphic services to the department;

Directorate: Ethnology, whose mission is to promote the development process in South Africa by providing ethnological and sociological assistance to government departments and to regional governments.

Over the past year, the Directorate of Office Administration has been establishing policy guidelines regarding recruitment and utilisation of personnel and strategic planning in the labour relations field with the aim of developing a labour relations monitoring system.

In January 1993, after the period of strategic planning, the Department formally adopted a policy of making its staff more representative of the population of South Africa. Mr Hoffman was a main player in advocating this policy; he knew that the best way for each component of the department to make its staff more representative was to take its cue from its client base. He was proud that this policy had been adopted and that each directorate was taking steps to ensure that, over a period of time, its staff composition would exactly mirror its client base. "The ideal situation," he explains, "is to have departmental employees serving their own people. After all, they know best the needs of their people." The department had gone through a rigorous exercise of identifying posts that could be filled by people of appropriate race. The outcome varied for each directorate, as each had a different client base. He knew, for instance, that the Chief Directorate for Industrial Development would have to be representative of the industrialists whom the directorate encourages to settle in particular areas. If the industrialists turned out to be, say, 80% white, then the ideal situation would be to have a staff component which was 80% white.

The Directorate for Development Planning was one of the directorates which had been targeted for recruitment of black people as its client base was largely black, and, conveniently, there were a number of vacancies within it.

As a personnel expert within a government department, Mr Hoffman was well aware of the personnel recruitment policies and procedures laid down by the Commission for Administration (CFA), the central personnel organisation for the Public Service. He had, over the years, been involved in the promotion of many people within the department. He was confident in the CFA's role as the guardian of the *merit and efficiency principle* which ensured that, within the public service, the post would always be awarded to the most suitable applicant. He knew that the 700 000-strong public service staff were protected by this statutory watch-dog body which ensured departmental compliance with the Public Service Act. He was confident that like everyone else in his department, he had been selected because he was the best person for the job. The CFA ensured, too, that fairness was applied with regard to promotional ranks within the public service, through ensuring compliance with the principles of seniority and merit. In terms of the seniority principles, when a number of people within the same grade applied for a more senior post, the candidate with the most seniority, determined by date of entry to the ranks, would take precedence.

In awarding promotion, he was also guided by the merit assessments which were carried out annually by the departments concerned but which were kept in a consolidated list by the CFA. He viewed this personnel evaluation procedure as an important aid to management in achieving the optimal utilisation of available manpower and a more efficient Public Service. In terms of this evaluation, employees are categorised according to merit; each merit category contains a seniority list. These lists helped Mr Hoffman draw up a prioritised list of people applying for a promotion level position. Usually the most senior person in the highest merit category would be put forward to the CFA for promotion approval. If the Head of Department felt that a person in a lower merit category or lower in seniority was the best person for the job, he would have to put a very convincing argument to the CFA validating this choice. Mr Hoffman had not done this very often but he knew how complicated and time consuming the process was. A thorough motivation had to be produced and often the resulting document would travel backwards and forwards between departments and the CFA for months on end before a final decision was made.

Many of the available positions were in the promotional ranks and, as such, Mr Hoffman was governed in his choices by CFA directives. Usually suitable candidates for such positions were sought amongst existing staff. This ensured that newcomers could not block the career paths of serving officials. This important protection is enshrined in article 10 of the Public Service Act. Existing civil servants knew that they had first option on positions advertised in a weekly publication put out by the CFA. Mr Hoffman wondered how he was going to recruit black people for these positions as well as adhere to CFA policy regarding promotional posts.

In January 1993, Mr Hoffman decided that, in order to attract suitable candidates for available positions, he would place advertisements in newspapers such as the Sowetan as well as advertising internally. Applications from black candidates poured in, many from well qualified candidates. Applicants were shortlisted and interviews were conducted.

A few months later, the department received a directive from top management to look at the department budget anew to see where expenditure could be trimmed. The directive had come to Mr Hoffman as, in a department of that nature, the biggest expenditure was personnel and the only way to trim costs was to reduce the number of posts in the department. Mr Hoffman was given the task of coordinating this difficult task. He wondered how he could carry it out without seriously impacting on the ability of the department to function and while attempting to make the staff more representative of its client base.

The obvious place to begin was with vacant positions. The department had a total of 2 670 established posts, of which 160 were vacant. There were a total of 320 black employees in the department, very few of whom, to his knowledge, qualified for entry into the promotional ranks. Mr Hoffman directed all components of the department to suspend the filling of posts until they had decided which posts could be cut. Each component was to put forward proposals to the chief executive for consideration, who would then take up the matter with the minister concerned.

This process was time-consuming. Mr Hoffman and the department were struggling to reconcile the two directives: to cut back on posts as well as make their staff complement more racially representative. It seemed an impossible task unless there were mass resignations, which appeared unlikely.

Vicky's phone call had made Mr Hoffman realise that the dilemma facing the department was affecting people's lives and he decided to investigate her case more fully.

VICKY RAMARUMO'S STORY

Vicky had recently graduated from Wits with a Higher Diploma in Development Planning. Ten years earlier she had completed a Masters in Public Administration, but after many years of working in various government departments in Bophuthatswana, she had felt the need to take a course which would hone her skills and provide her with the opportunity to specialise.

Vicky was very excited to see a government department advertising in the *Sowetan* for someone with her qualifications. She saw this as a sign that the government was seriously attempting to open up its recruitment to groups previously excluded. She phoned for the required application forms, filled them out carefully and sent them off with apprehension. She knew her qualifications and experience made her an ideal candidate for the position but she wondered how an application from a black woman would be received by the department concerned.

A few weeks later, Vicky received 12 hours' notice to attend an interview. She really wanted this position, with the security it offered, and was put out that she had been given so little notice to prepare for the interview. She survived the gruelling session and afterwards felt confident that she had impressed the tough but fair panel, and particularly the Director of the relevant component, Mr Jacobs. She felt suited to the position and given the positive response she had received at the interview, sensed that the job was within her grasp.

Vicky's positive feeling was vindicated when she received a telephone call from Mr Jacobs: "You have made it through the interview and I would like to work with you," was his message. Vicky was elated: all her hard work and years of study were finally paying off. A few days later Mr Jacobs again phoned her to enquire about a suitable starting date and by the end of March Jacobs confirmed that the Commission for Administration had set the 15th April as an appropriate time to start. Although Vicky had worked in the Bophuthatswana Development Corporation for a number of years she had never worked for a South African State Department. Concerned about orienting herself in this new environment, she phoned Mr Jacobs to enquire whether he would be prepared to meet her in order to go over a few of her concerns. He readily agreed and a meeting was set up. At this meeting Jacobs explained the structure of the Department by drawing up an organisational chart and indicated that because of her number of years' experience, she would be slotted into the position as Senior Planner. He outlined the salary scales within the department as well as the experience needed for particular staff levels (see below).

Benefits seemed good and included a car allowance. Jacobs recommended that she find herself a flat closer to the offices and transfer her children to a nearby school so that travelling would not be such a problem. Vicky was happy with the offer made to her and waited patiently for her letter of appointment to arrive in the post.

As the weeks wore on, Vicky had a growing sense that something was wrong. By the 14th April Vicky still had not received the promised letter. Anxiously, she phoned Jacobs, who told her that her file was still with the Commission but that he would phone her in a few days and that she should be ready to start immediately.

By the end of April, 15 days after she was due to take up employment with the Department, Vicky had not received her letter of appointment. She phoned again, only to be informed bluntly that Jacobs had resigned. Shocked and worried, Vicky enquired about the status of her application and was told that his office was no longer dealing with her file and that it had been passed on to the personnel department and was in the hands of a Mr Van der Walt.

Mr Van der Walt advised Vicky that the delay in her application was due to the Commission for Administration returning her file as there was a candidate for the position of Deputy Director who was already employed by the state and they had to wait on his department to submit his merit assessment report before they could decide on the final appointment. Vicky could not understand what this had to do with her appointment as she was not competing for the position mentioned. She felt she was being fobbed off.

On 1st June, Vicky again phoned the department. As she was to relate some time later, "All they said to me was 'Oh! I see! You are one of the people who are supposed to start work today or tomorrow', but no-one could help me or tell me what was going on, so I decided to make a trip to Pretoria to see them, face to face!"

On 3rd June Vicky visited Mr Van der Walt's office at 08:30, where he insisted that there was nothing that could be done until the evaluation report on the other candidate had been received. His superior, Ms Muller agreed but left the office and later returned with a document which confirmed that Mr Jacobs had verbally directed Vicky to start work on 15 April. Her attitude towards Vicky visibly softened after this, although she would not let Vicky have a copy of the document. By 15:30, Ms Muller, although "not promising anything", confirmed that, as the personnel department, they had the power to appoint Vicky *provided Mr Du Pisane, the Director General of the Directorate of Development Planning, was prepared to work with her.*

Ms Muller arranged an appointment for Vicky with Mr Du Pisane for the following morning. Mr Du Pisane's secretary was polite enough and offered Vicky a seat and a cup of tea. Mr Du Pisane was a different story. When he arrived he went straight into his office without acknowledging Vicky. Then he returned to tell Vicky that she should not be sitting where she was, but to wait in the hallway. He instructed his secretary to call Ms Muller so he could talk to her. Shortly after that, Ms Muller entered Mr Du Pisane's office and the door promptly slammed shut behind them. Nevertheless, Vicky could hear much table-banging and loud talking. When they re-emerged, Ms Muller looked upset and her face was flushed. Mr Du Pisane told Vicky that the matter was being handled by the Commission for Administration and there was nothing more to be said about it. Distraught and feeling powerless, Vicky asked for a contact person in the CFA and was told to talk to a Ms Botha. She telephoned Ms Botha, who seemed ready to help, and they agreed to meet at 14:00.

During the interview, Ms Botha agreed to phone Ms Muller in order to get some answers. Ms Muller explained that although the department had the right to appoint Vicky, as the position she was applying for was below Deputy Director level, they would have to wait for the merit evaluation report on the person applying for the position as Deputy Director before the issue could be resolved. This seemed like the end to Vicky, and tears began to roll down her face. She could not understand what the applicant for the position of Deputy Director had to do with her and could only assume that the treatment she had received had something to do with the fact that she was a black woman who spoke English and not Afrikaans. It seemed like a hopeless situation. As she said later, "I was discouraged. I felt humiliated, cheated, robbed of my rights. I had a miserable weekend. I did not know what I was going to tell my kids. I wondered where my God was at this point."

Vicky made one last attempt to get some answers and demanded to see Mr du Pisane. When she entered his office it was clear that he had been warned that a very angry woman was on her way to see him. He sat stony-faced across the desk from Vicky:, "You arranged to meet me," he barked, "I am not going to say anything – you are going to do the talking."

Vicky launched into her story and told him about her appointment commencing 15 April. He retorted, "Go and look for a person who has appointed you; I have nothing to do with you. It's like coming to me and asking me about finance when I am not a banker or about welfare issues when I am not a welfare officer." After more angry words, and failing to get anywhere, she left. In the corridor, she bumped into two employees, a white woman and a black man who told her that she was lucky that Mr Du Pisane had agreed to see her but that there was no way in the world that he was going to allow her to work with him.

By early July, Vicky heard that Mr Du Pisane had collected all the application files from the Commission for Administration, as he planned to reduce the number of appointments resulting from the original advertisement because of budget constraints. She knew then that she was fighting a losing battle. For months she had been walking endless Kafkaesque corridors entangled in the proverbial red tape. She had stopped looking for a job when Mr Jacobs had offered her the Chief Planner position over the telephone and had thus lost precious time and countless opportunities while waiting in vain for the department to take decisions which affected her future. She fully intended to take the department to court, and she had just let Mr Hoffman know this in no uncertain terms.

MR HOFFMAN'S DILEMMA

Mr Hoffman knew that he faced a number of challenges. He had been charged with the task of making the department's staff composition more racially representative against a background of shrinking resources. He also had to operate within the context of existing CFA policies and procedures. Trying to reconcile these three elements had taken far too long and valuable applicants were being lost as a result. Now his department was facing legal action from a young woman who had at one point been considered a serious contender for the position as Senior Planner. There seemed to be no easy solutions. He put his head down in the crook of his arm resting on the desk and sighed. None of the personnel books lining his office walls were of any assistance. In any case, this was no textbook situation – there were too many variables involved. He leaned back in his executive chair, folded his arms and thought long and hard. Suddenly he stood up and strode out of his office – he had had an idea!

BACKGROUND INFORMATION

Table 1: *Staff Levels in the Directorate of Development Planning*

POSITION	EXPERIENCE	REMUNERATION
Director	4-year degree + 14 years' experience	R105 000
Deputy Director	4-year degree + 12 years' experience	R85 000
Planners:		
Chief Planner	4-year degree + 9.5 years' experience	R75 000
Senior Planner	4-year degree + 7.5 years' experience	R60 000
Planner	4-year degree + 3 years' experience	R50 000
Assistant Planner	4-year degree + 0 years' experience	R26 000

CASE STUDY THREE

KARL SMITH, ADAM MARKSWALA AND PRAGMATISM IN GOVERNMENT PLANNING

Erwin Schwella

Adam Markswala, the Minister of Human Resources, is facing a potential powder-keg. During the recent election campaign which brought the Liberation Movement Party to power, promises were made to labour movements with regard to minimum wages and other concessions, but there has been little movement on this front over the past couple of months. The minister is aware that at a recent national conference of the Farm and Allied Workers Association (FAWA), a resolution was accepted to: "put pressure on government to move ahead with the improvement of the plight of farm workers". On top of this, just last week, a group of domestic workers presented him with a petition to: "remind government about election promises to domestic workers". Action would have to be taken immediately to avoid a crisis of confidence in the new government. He knew just the person to take that action: Jane Februarie, the Chief Director of Policy Research in the department.

BACKGROUND

The Republic of Newsa came into being after a period of struggle and long and difficult negotiations. The Liberation Movement Party (LMP) had come to power polling 50,6% of the total vote with a corresponding 202 seats in a Parliament of 400 members. The main opposition party, the Newsa National Party (NNP), polled 26% of the total vote but formed a loose alliance with other parties, thereby giving it control over approximately 140 of 400 parliamentary seats or about 35% of the seats in Parliament. The new constitution provides for an executive consisting of a president and a cabinet of 15 ministers taking executive responsibility for a corresponding number of government departments.

The Constitution of Newsa incorporates a Bill of Rights providing for basic human rights for all the people of Newsa. The Constitution also includes clauses catering for affirmative action in government policies, programmes and employment. The LMP has developed policies favouring an active role for the state in development, such as the provision of housing, education and health services, so that all citizens should have access to these services in an equitable way. Simultaneously, policies that address the great historical inequalities in the Newsa society, are being pursued.

The Department of Manpower was replaced, in the new government, by the Department of Human Resources. The Minister of Human Resources is the main political office-bearer of the Department and has responsibility for:
- labour relations;
- basic conditions of service;
- job creation programmes; and
- national human resource planning.

THE PEOPLE INVOLVED

Adam Markswala, Minister of Human Resources, is a seasoned politician with a serious commitment to development and the redress of disparities brought about by previous discriminatory laws and practices in the labour field.

During an uprising against the oppressive regime in 1976, Minister Markswala had been a student at the Northern University studying political anthropology and sociology. As a prominent student leader he was soon in conflict with the Oldsa Police and was held for long periods without trial in terms of the then existing Security Act. During these periods, he was vigorously questioned and – on occasion – assaulted and subjected to serious physical and psychological stress. During one of his periods of freedom he crossed the borders and joined the exiled community in a neighbouring state. Here he made rapid political progress and was awarded an international study grant to further his studies at a British university. He completed an undergraduate degree in economics and politics at this university and was then selected to do graduate work at a university in East Berlin in the former German Democratic Republic (East Germany). He graduated at the age of 34, with a Master's degree in economic planning, and went on to undertake a number of internships in government departments in countries in the former Eastern Bloc. He subsequently joined the exiled bureaucracy of the LMP in its Vienna office during 1989.

Mr Markswala returned to Oldsa after the dramatic announcements on the 2nd of February 1990 and the unbanning of opposition political organisations such as the LMP. He later became involved in the negotiation process as an adviser to the LMP and was also part of a team co-ordinating research into a new macro-economic policy for the LMP.

He was nominated as an LMP candidate in the first democratic elections during 1994 and after his party's resounding victory, took a seat in the first parliament of Newsa. In Parliament he impressed all with his zeal and commitment. He contributed in an insightful way to debates on the future of the economy of Newsa. On numerous occasions he stressed that Newsaners should not forget the past, but that reconciliation and constructive effort were of paramount importance for sustained peace and development in the Republic of Newsa. It came as no surprise when he was appointed to cabinet as Minister of Human Resources after an executive reshuffle during 1996.

Karl Smith, the Permanent Secretary of the Department of Human Resources, is a career official with impeccable professional credentials and academic background, having served for many years in the civil service of the Oldsa Republic. After studying law at the Oldsa Indian Ocean University he joined the then Department of Justice, where he completed his pupilage to be admitted as an advocate. He subsequently transferred to the former Department of Labour, where he was involved in providing technical advice on the formulation of a new labour dispensation for Oldsa. He drafted many of the bills which reformed the Oldsa labour dispensation, allowing workers freedom of association and trade union rights.

Once the new labour legislation was firmly in place, he was given the opportunity to study an MBA specialising in labour relations at the Business School of Southern Liberal English University. Throughout his intensive course work he was convinced of the importance of allowing free markets to settle questions of supply, demand and distribution in any modern economy. His Master's dissertation was titled: "Market forces and productivity: invisible hands for improving national growth". By all accounts it was an excellent piece of academic work and he obtained the MBA degree with a first-class pass.

His obvious talents led to regular promotions within the Department of Labour. He often contributed to international academic conferences and journals on labour matters. Although he was never a member of a political party – and thought that this was the preferred position for any senior government official – he held firm and serious views on individual freedom and believed that any form of discrimination, whether social or in the labour market, impinged upon the proper functioning of market forces.

At the time of the elections of 1994 he was held in high esteem by international labour experts and was also well known and respected by the broad labour movement, with whose leaders he had had regular and cordial contact over many years. When the then Director General of the Department of Labour retired, he was the obvious choice for the newly created position of Permanent Secretary, Department of Human Resources, and was appointed to this position on 1 January 1995.

During his first year of office many changes took place in the Department. The new government showed that it was serious about introducing policies and programmes to involve the State in a more active way in the labour field. Three developments were of particular importance:

- the government pledged itself to wealth taxes in order to raise money for job creation in areas such as self-help housing schemes;
- the government pledged itself to enhancing living conditions through regulation of labour matters such as minimum wages and conditions of service;
- a programme of affirmative action was instituted for government employees.

Under the programme of affirmative action a number of new appointments were made to the Department, including two black Newsaners to the joint positions of Deputy Permanent Secretary and a brown Newsaner to the position of Chief Director: Policy Research.

Jane Februarie assumed duties as Chief Director: Policy Research in the Department of Human Resources on 1 July 1995. Although it was known that she was a beneficiary of the affirmative action programme of the Department, she was a highly meritorious appointee with tremendous potential. Admittedly, she had jumped from the position of Assistant Director straight into the position of Chief Director, thus skipping the two civil service grades of Deputy Director and Director.

Jane started her working career in 1970 as a clerk in the Department of Coloured Affairs of Oldsa after passing Standard 10. She came from a poor rural family and grew up in the Boland. Her father was a bricklayer who suffered from recurring tuberculosis, and her mother was a proud woman who worked as a shop assistant and supplemented the meagre family income by taking in laundry which she washed and ironed in the evenings and over weekends. She offered constant encouragement to her four children and she asked of them only that that they should achieve an educational level of at least a school leaving certificate or Standard 10. She instilled in them a healthy pride and idealism.

Soon after starting her first job, Jane decided to study further. She enrolled with the SA Correspondence Technikon for a Diploma in State Finance which she completed in 1976. Subsequently she enrolled for degree studies at the extramural division of South Western Cape University, from which she graduated with a commerce degree, majoring in Business Economics and Accountancy.

From 1987 to 1989, Jane was enrolled for the MPA degree at Southern Afrikaans University. The course work for this degree stressed open systems theory and contingency management; strategic thinking and management in accordance with trends in the political, economic and social environments. It also promoted the values of legitimacy, effectiveness and efficiency and caring in governance and public management. The course used managerial pragmatism rather than ideological rigidity as its philosophical point of departure. Jane found that the theoretical and conceptual content of the course provided her with a better understanding of her functions as a government manager as well as useful techniques for improving her technical capacity as a manager. She specialised in Policy Analysis, and in 1989, was awarded her MPA with excellent marks.

Promotion possibilities for Jane in the Oldsa civil service were generally limited to so-called "own affairs" departments. However Jane gradually scaled the promotion ladder through the clerical ranks, reaching the administrative ranks in the course of the 1980s. After obtaining her MPA degree she was transferred to the newly established labour relations section of the Own Affairs Administration. Initially she was bestowed with responsibilities equal to the post of Assistant Director but without formal appointment, or appropriate remuneration or benefits. She felt sure that any male in a similar situation would have been awarded full status albeit for a probationary period but decided, in typical fashion, to accept the situation as a challenge. In due course she was permanently appointed to the position, which she found very challenging during the period of civil service restructuring and simultaneous unionisation. Jane served competently and impressed her colleagues with her sophisticated approach to labour negotiations.

As part of the process of affirmative action in the Newsa civil service, talented civil servants who had previously been excluded from senior positions were head-hunted for promotion. Jane was an obvious choice on the basis of her merit, qualifications and potential, although she would not have complied with the experience requirements under the previous dispensation. She was selected provisionally and had to undergo extensive screening tests, including a three-day assessment centre evaluation. She qualified with flying colours and was appointed as Chief Director: Policy, commencing duty on 1 July 1995.

Her initial reception in the ministry was ostensibly cordial but she soon became aware that the Permanent Secretary, Karl Smith, had difficulty accepting the implementation of the affirmative action programme. He explained to her that he had no personal grudges against women or blacks as employees but that he believed that affirmative action constituted an unwarranted interference with the labour market. This created the possibility of "reverse discrimination" with which he could not agree in principle. He also took care to stress that he only expected the highest standards of professional conduct and that no allowances would be made for mistakes made due to inexperience or lack of training. Standards had to be maintained at all costs and people had to accept responsibility for their own development. After this confrontation, he treated her with distant courtesy.

One of Jane's colleagues, a newly appointed Deputy Permanent Secretary, Mr Mpiso, was very supportive and understanding. Jane and Mr Mpiso often got together to discuss work-related problems and to test new ideas and possible actions.

Mr Mpike, the other newly appointed Deputy Permanent Secretary, was less supportive. During a conference which he and Jane attended at a hotel in Durban, he invited her to dinner after which he suggested drinks in his room. Jane refused. Subsequently Mr Mpike indicated that he was disappointed with some of the reports Jane submitted to him. These same reports were, however, acceptable to Mr Mpiso and the Permanent Secretary. One of the reports criticised by Mr Mpike drew commending comments from the Minister, Mr Markswala.

THE MEETING

Today is the 3rd of March 1996. Parliament is in session and the legislative process to implement the policy agendas and proposals of the new government is in full swing. Following on from election promises made by the ruling LMP, and the subsequent demands made by labour organisations, Jane Februarie has been requested by the Minister of Human Resources to investigate the implications of the introduction of minimum wage legislation. As a first step she has arranged a meeting between the Permanent Secretary, the two Deputy Permanent Secretaries, herself and the Minister, to be held at 09:15.

The Minister: *"Good morning, colleagues! I hope you are all well and ready for this important meeting. I want to thank Ms Februarie for her effort in arranging this* meeting about the very relevant topic of minimum wages for our people, who were previously exploited under the system of apartheid. I think we shall proceed by providing an opportunity for all present to briefly make introductory statements about their understanding of the situation and what should be done about it.

"Let me start with the needs of government. You will realise that this policy proposal has to take into account the material base of our society as well as the historical oppression of the people: mere equal opportunity will not suffice. An equitable solution requires policies which will really make a difference. Bear in mind that government has to show progress in its task of development. The policies also have to be acceptable to the trade union movement.

"Government is therefore very keen to set minimum wages for farm labourers and domestic workers. The acts to be made in this regard should be very clear, unambiguous and enforceable. The minimum wages for these particular industries should be set at a level that is at least 40% above the current average. Government believes that the Act should be an empowering one giving the Minister the discretion to set the minimum wage levels from time to time as he or she may deem fit.

"Furthermore, time is of the essence. Government wants draft legislation prepared as soon as possible so that the matter can be settled during this Parliamentary session. The people have suffered long enough! Any comments?"

Jane Februarie noticed that Karl Smith was energetically making notes during the Minister's address. Her other two colleagues listened attentively and Jane had a feeling that sparks were going to fly. She waited expectantly for Mr Mpike to speak.

Deputy Permanent Secretary, Mr Mpike: "Mr Minister, I agree with all that you have said and want to add my support to the points you made so well as usual. There is, however, a matter I would like to raise and that is a process matter. We all know the needs of our people and how urgent they are. While they are suffering we hold long drawn-out meetings such as this one. I believe it is abundantly clear what the needs are and you have already provided the solutions. I think we should have much more action than idle talk around here. I am continuously confronted with masses of paper in the form of reports and time-consuming meetings while people go hungry out there. There seems to be too much intellectual and elitist ping-ponging in our Department. I want action as the people cannot eat, nor sleep in, papers, reports and meetings. I believe we should seriously encourage Ms Februarie to try and cut down on all this quasi-intellectualism."

Deputy Permanent Secretary, Mr Mpiso: "Mr Minister, I would urge us to be serious about the analysis of the situation. I believe there are many and complicated factors to be taken into account when deciding on the principle and possible amount of minimum wages. I think it is very necessary that we should have a proper investigation of all the factors involved and come up with a well-reasoned approach. This need not take a long time, either.

"We have an excellent person in Ms Februarie, who has extensive organisational capacity and access to a network of researchers in and outside the Department. I believe we should design a programme with a time schedule to investigate the matter properly and that we can set this schedule in such a way that critical deadlines and the needs of government will be satisfied.

"I understand and have empathy with the needs of our people but over-hasty action can easily create more suffering in the medium and long term. I do think Ms Februarie has shown her capacity to manage and co-ordinate projects like these and I propose we give her about three weeks to commission research and submit proposals to a meeting of ourselves again."

Jane Februarie: "Mr Minister and colleagues, the policy of government in respect of minimum wages is a very important and, I believe, a necessary one given the political and socio-economic realities of our society. At the same time we have to realise that the principle of minimum wages and especially the amounts involved will have effects on the sectors employing farm and domestic workers. It is known that these sectors in certain areas are very sensitive to the effects of increased labour costs.

"If the matter is not handled in a considered and analytical way, it may impact on the viability of certain industries and can also lead to overall decreases in employment levels. There are already trends indicating increased mechanisation of agricultural activities. These trends may be amplified if labour costs rise too dramatically. On the other hand it is also known through research that some increases will be affordable and sustainable in these sectors. The challenge is to find the correct levels given all circumstances.

"It is possible to investigate the matter from a technical angle and such investigation need not take too long as we can co-ordinate the collection of the data and researchers. I am keen to assist in such a process if that is what is decided here today. I also believe that I can come up with a first report in the three weeks mentioned by Mr Mpiso."

Jane Februarie looks around and sees that Karl Smith is ready to fire away.

Permanent Secretary, Mr Karl Smith: "I would like to agree with our colleague, Mr Mpike, that we have too many meetings about certain matters. I want to suggest that this meeting is one of those that are superfluous.

"We have created a system of labour relations through labour legislation which is regarded as the most advanced in the world. Under this legislation it is possible for employers and employees to associate freely in structures such as employer organisations and trade unions. This enables these interest groups to bargain collectively to find the correct levels of remuneration and service benefits through negotiation. If the parties are not able to come to consensus about these matters there are further structures such as industrial councils, arbitration bodies and the Industrial Court which can settle disputes in a just and equitable way.

"The structures and processes I have just mentioned already impede the complete freedom of the labour market and it has been argued that unions have so much power in the collective bargaining process that they force salary and benefit packages to levels that are too high. This affects the prices of products, services and the inflation rate. The net result is a weaker economy, less productivity and decreased international competitiveness. In the end this could lead to more unemployment and sustained poverty and deprivation. I have, however, reluctantly resigned myself to this interference in the free market of labour.

"The involvement of the State in this meddling way by introducing minimum wages I can **never** agree with! It will of necessity lead to the same and even harsher consequences than the unionisation of labour. It has the capacity to decimate whole industries, with dire consequences for productive forces. The people who are supposed to gain will inevitably be the greatest losers. I view any attempts in this regard as futile, inherently dangerous and even unwise! I wish to further ...."

At this point the minister interrupts:

"Mr Smith, we are in real need of good policies. We cannot reduce suffering human beings to commodities and units of production any longer. The people are expecting us to improve their living conditions. I find your position problematic and I will have to report your intransigence to Cabinet! I have to leave now for my next meeting scheduled in five minutes, but we will talk again."

The minister pushes back his chair and leaves. In the stunned silence that follows, Jane ponders these points:

- How did we get into this mess?
- What explains what happened here?
- Could I have done something differently to avoid this situation? and
- How am I going to get this process back on track?

CASE STUDY FOUR

A PRINCIPAL, A VISION AND CHANGE IN AN UNCOMPROMISING COMMUNITY: PART I

Sipho Sithole

It was back in 1980 that Mr J. J. Poto, the vice-principal of Ukhetho High School in one of Natal's townships, received a brown envelope marked *amptelik/official/eyombuso*. He wondered what is was that he had done wrong. As he opened it, his hands began to sweat. As far as he could remember, the last time he had received an official letter was several years back when he was a junior teacher; he had gone on vacation and had stayed away three days longer than he was supposed to. As a result, he had received a warning from the Department of Education and Culture for what was considered misconduct. He was not aware of anything he had done recently which could be called misconduct, but could think of no other reason why he should receive an official letter. He tore open the envelope with shaking hands and read the first sentence which began: "The Minister of Education would like to congratulate you on your appointment as...," Mr Poto sighed with great relief. He had been appointed principal of Malandela High School, in the same township as Ukhetho.

He knew in his heart that he deserved this appointment. He had a vision of what a school should look like, and for years had longed to implement that vision. He had often argued with his colleagues in the staff room that Ukhetho High School should shift from being a craft-and-skills school towards being a technology-oriented institution. But, since he was not the principal of the school, and couldn't offer any convincing solution when he was asked by his colleagues how he would adapt a government-run school to his ideal, he had never pursued his ideas. But now, finally, he had the opportunity to prove that it could be done! Malandela High school would soon resemble the vision he had for so long held for Ukhetho High school. His appointment was a dream come true.

AN UNCOMPROMISING ENVIRONMENT

Upon assuming his duties as school principal, Mr Poto realised that he had a long battle ahead of him. Like any other African school in the township, Malandela High School (as it was known then) was a typical U-shaped structure, with all the classrooms, and the principal's office, the staff room, and toilets for staff and students crammed into the three blocks. It was overcrowded and under-resourced.

Ever since learning about his appointment, Mr Poto had spent sleepless nights thinking about how he would transform Malandela High into the kind of school which would produce children able to take advantage of South Africa's potential as an industrialising country. He knew that the shortage of skilled workers contributed significantly to the nation's inability to build and maintain a strong economy and to keep pace and compete effectively with other industrialised countries. At every level of activity there were insufficient highly trained and competent individuals to perform the functions necessary to the country's economic development. He knew that the curriculum offered by black schools, informed as it was by apartheid policy, had been designed to produce a semi-skilled labour force for the purpose of serving the capitalist economy at the lowest possible cost. It was, therefore, inadequate to meet the needs of commerce and industry.

The biggest challenge, as Mr Poto saw it, was that of re-instilling a culture of learning into the school. Mr Poto believed that resistance to, and the rejection of apartheid education, which had reached its peak by the early eighties, was justified. However he felt that it had led to a crisis in African schools, where the very will to learn had been destroyed. As for the prevailing low standards in African schools, Mr Poto believed they were a function of several factors such as: wholly inadequate government funding; a continuous increase in the number of pupils enrolling every year without an equivalent increase in the number of teachers, which resulted in overcrowded classrooms; poor teacher training facilities and a scarcity of properly qualified teachers, resulting in poor standards of teaching. Furthermore, the emphasis in African schools was on practical subjects which were perceived as qualifying students only for manual occupations and therefore rejected by many of them. Yet all this was small challenge to Mr Poto compared with the complex political environment in which he found himself.

Many school inspectors and principals in schools controlled by the KwaZulu government were members of Inkatha, some of them by choice and some by virtue of being employees of the KwaZulu government, where Inkatha 'called the shots'. Those who found themselves in the latter situation still could not afford to be seen openly aligning themselves with the Mass Democratic Movement (MDM), since that would jeopardise their positions.

Upon his appointment as principal of Malandela, Mr Poto had been requested to sign a pledge, sent by the KwaZulu government, to the effect that he would not criticise that Government, its leaders or, obviously, Inkatha. Failure to sign would have meant rejecting the appointment as principal, something Mr Poto could not do. Furthermore, the local MP for the KwaZulu Legislative Assembly and member of Inkatha's central committee asserted control at all schools and went in and out of school principals' offices as if he owned the schools. The KwaZulu Department of Education and Culture, Mr Poto's employer, was at logger-heads with the MDM aligned student movement. The students' struggle against apartheid education and Inkatha's control over education at the school and community levels, was to lead to violent confrontations. Vigilantes loyal to Inkatha patrolled the school, often chasing and attacking those students who were sympathetic to the MDM.

Mr Poto realised that if he was to effect change in this environment of escalating violence, he would have to convince everyone that the changes he wanted to make would have a positive impact on the community as a whole. He would have to be careful, however, particularly as he himself was seen as part of the structure of apartheid.

Despite the unfavourable circumstances under which he had to work, Mr Poto was determined not to be discouraged. Such causes of the education crisis as overcrowded classrooms, a lack of books and other learning resources, unqualified teachers, the high drop-out and failure rates in schools, and above all, the inadequacy of the education provided for Africans, all demanded immediate attention. He decided to tackle the last of these issues first: by changing the curriculum offered by his school, to bring it in line with the needs of potential employers of his students.

CONSULTATION FOR A NEW CURRICULUM

In an effort to gain a realistic picture of the kind of skills and qualifications that would be most useful in the South African economy, Mr Poto decided to talk to representatives of key sectors of the local economy: representatives of private enterprise, the Durban Metropolitan Chamber, and industrial institutions. An understanding of science, an ability to reason scientifically and mathematically and to solve problems rationally were skills stressed by industry. In the course of his meetings, Mr Poto was promised financial, material and other support by private concerns in industry and commerce.

A drastic change in the school curriculum would be needed to turn the school into a technology-oriented institution. Mr Poto felt that subjects offered should fall into four categories: commerce, science, general, as well as technical subjects such as woodwork, welding and metal work, building science, electrical science, motor mechanics, engineering drawing and so on.

In order to introduce this new curriculum, however, Mr Poto needed appropriate human resources. In common with many African schools, the teaching staff at Malandela was not fully qualified nor sufficiently trained to offer the kind of education that Mr Poto had in mind. Of the 12 teachers on the existing staff, four lacked teaching certificates. Some of the teachers had been teaching at the school for a number of years; many unfortunately taught subjects that Mr Poto saw as "useless and not contributing to the needs of the industry and society as a whole". Already murmurs of dissatisfaction could be heard in the corridors as teachers feared that they would be transferred elsewhere and replaced. Obviously change was not going to be accepted very easily, but Mr Poto would have to find a way to win the co-operation of his staff. He wondered if they could be retrained to teach the subjects he wanted to introduce.

Another challenge facing Mr Poto was how to involve the community in the new school model. Should he, an employee of the KwaZulu government, risk consulting the political, trade union and student organisations about the type of change and the new approach to education that he envisaged? The KwaZulu government, through various organs, asserted control at school level, preventing the formation of student representative councils (SRCs) and parent-teacher-student associations (PTSAs) and other educational movements with the exception of the Natal African Teachers Union (an Inkatha affiliate). After consideration, he decided that consulting with structures which were regarded as pro-ANC, would be political suicide.

HOW TO REALISE THE DREAM?

Nevertheless, he was convinced that, before he could implement changes, he would need to consult with and gain the endorsement of all concerned. To add to his troubles, three visiting education officials from Pretoria indicated that central bureaucracy disapproved of the idea of a comprehensive high school in the middle of the township. Given all the obstacles he faced, Mr Poto wondered how he would ever realise his dream.

CASE STUDY FIVE

A PRINCIPAL, A VISION AND CHANGE IN AN UNCOMPROMISING COMMUNITY: PART II

Sipho Sithole

In Part I we saw Mr Poto engage himself in gathering information from industry in order to establish what kind of skills and qualifications would be most useful in an industrialised country. This enquiry confirmed Mr Poto's suspicions: that the school curriculum offered at Malandela High was irrelevant to the needs of commerce and industry, where there was a shortage of skilled workers at all levels. Mr Poto has set himself the task of transforming Malandela High from a craft school into an institution with a technological orientation.

FUNDING

Mr Poto sought financial and material support from the industrial sector for his new approach to education, promising potential sponsors that he could produce students with the right skills if given the opportunity. He did not rely solely on the private sector, but also established a development fund for the school with the help of the parents and the staff, towards which everybody contributed.

Mr Poto's clear vision of how he could meet the demands of the industrial sector impressed many companies. Natal Spices, the first donor, had provided the first block of classrooms back in 1982. Both students and the principal were so keen to see progress that they could not wait for the contractor to begin work on the new block; instead, they put on their overalls and started digging the foundations for the building.

Home Cooking Inc., with its interest in Home Economics, a subject to be offered by the school, also donated equipment and financial support. Other sponsors such as Bankrupt Bank (now Last National Bank), African Exploiters Chemical Industries (AECI), Town Crook Inc., and Toys South Africa, followed suit.

Mr Poto was amazed by the rapid progress that he was making in getting donor support. Major contractors had begun to sub-contract some of their projects to keep up with the inflow of financial support that resulted in the mushrooming of buildings to left and right, in front of and behind the original school blocks.

STAFFING

As more staff was needed, Mr Poto started advertising vacancies in a local newspaper. Malandela High needed staff committed to Mr Poto's vision and this included all levels of staff right from administrators, clerks, typists, and receptionist, as well as teachers. Mr Poto did not want to go wrong when choosing selection methods. What worried Mr Poto was that senior appointments would be made by the KwaZulu Department of Education and Culture and as such, would be outside Mr Poto's jurisdiction. Where he could, however, he decided to include his teachers in the interview panels. He wanted his staff to feel as if they had a real stake in the school and he thought inclusion of staff members would prevent any resentments building up over the appointment of so many new staff members. This approach was very different to previous recruitment strategies followed by the school when the headmaster alone decided on appointments.

Applicants were subsequently called in and faced a panel which consisted of the senior staff, senior management, chairman of the parents' committee, and inspectorate. Applications for vacancies, such as heads of department, were also invited from members of the existing staff who had to complete their application forms and thus compete with applicants from outside.

STAFF DEVELOPMENT

Even though Mr Poto had finally succeeded in putting together the right kind of staff, the problem of inherited unqualified and ill-trained staff still plagued him and demanded his attention. He knew that something had to been done to lessen the tension that was building up at school among those teachers who feared for their jobs. It was not his intention to retrench non-qualified staff; instead, he hoped to find ways of improving their skills and performance. Together with the staff, Mr Poto reflected on the way they as teachers presented their lessons to the students and identified some of the areas where improvement was needed. They identified the need to adapt themselves to a new situation by adopting a pupil-centred approach to education. The principal and the staff felt this was the only way that the school could produce independent thinking, creative students with the necessary problem-solving skills.

To produce that kind of student, the staff would have to be developed as well. It was in 1984 that the principal succeeded in persuading Toys South Africa to allocate funds for staff development. Mr Poto also felt the need for further training, as he realised that he lacked some of the skills essential for a school principal. Mr Poto felt that he had a good sense of the areas in which leaders in education needed to be trained and he could list a few: communication, delegation, listening skills, and fund raising, as well as good human relations and he emphasised the need to be a good PRO (public relations officer) in order to effectively communicate with the community. He decided, however, to ascertain from the staff themselves what they felt their needs were. The school invited a professor from one of the local universities to work with the staff on their development. The University of Zululand had also opened a branch in Umlazi Township back in

1979 which was now in full operation, and therefore some of the staff enrolled at Zululand University's Extra-Mural Studies Division. Umlazi College for Further Education was also used by some for staff development.

GOVERNING STRUCTURES

By the mid-eighties the school, by now called Malandela Comprehensive High School, had a formal governing and administrative structure. Mr Poto advocated a three-tier hierarchical administrative structure with two-way communication channels, composed of *senior management*, viz. the principal and three deputies, *middle management*, that is eleven heads of department, and the *lower level* which comprised unofficial senior and junior staff members. Mr Poto encouraged innovative and creative ideas from any member of the staff. Anybody was free to propose policies which could be reviewed by everybody and adopted if approved. For instance, HODs could suggest policies for their own departments which were subject to scrutiny and could be reviewed from time to time to ensure their continued relevance.

The governance structure was to be composed of the governing council, made up of parents, teachers, and members of the community. Mr Poto did not see the necessity to accommodate students in this structure as he saw their role as being confined to that of prefects and class captains. Neither Mr Poto nor the Department of Education made provision for the SRC or PTSAs, as they saw these structures as affiliated to the NECC, which in turn was affiliated to the UDF, and hence pro-ANC.

By 1985, a stranger in the area might easily have mistaken Malandela Comprehensive High for a university, hospital, teachers' college, or technikon, as it had become a huge complex comprising 11 new buildings in addition to the original U-shaped one.

The school employs 84 academic staff, has 1 460 students and offers close to 40 subjects, divided between commerce, science and general subjects, as well as technical subjects such as woodwork, welding and metalwork, building science, electrical science, motor mechanics, and technical drawing, to name but a few. Last year's matric pass rate was about 94%, of which 54% gained university entrance exemption.

TIME FOR REFLECTION

Even though Mr Poto seems happy and proud of his achievement, there was one incident which has left him scared. When speaking of it his jovial demeanour quickly turns to anger and his voice becomes stern. This incident was the assassination of lawyer and political activist, Mrs Victoria Mxenge, outside her home in Umlazi Township in August 1985. This slaying led to mass student uprisings, which spilled over to the entire community and resulted in confrontations between Inkatha and members of the Mass Democratic Movement, especially the youth.

Malandela Comprehensive High School was affected when the youth marched to the school singing *Saze sasihle isikole, kaze siyofike sithini kumama Mrs Mxenge*, meaning, 'Look how beautiful this school is, what are we going to say to our mother Mrs Mxenge?' According to Mr Poto, he confronted the angry youths, telling them Mrs Mxenge was an educated person who surely would have appreciated the progress that Malandela had achieved and its approach to education, as well as its attempt to foster a culture of learning in the community.

It was after this confrontation with the angry youths that an attempt was made on the lives of Mr Poto and his family. His house was bombed twice in 1986. To Mr Poto, this was an indication that the people lacked understanding as to what the school was trying to achieve. He points out that it was very difficult in the political climate of that time to achieve the desired objectives.

Looking at the present state of education in South Africa, Mr Poto identifies a number of important issues facing school managers today. These are the need for staff development, which should be an on-going process, and pupil development with the need to focus on an individual's overall record of achievement rather than isolated instances of success.

As Mr Poto reflects on the history of the Malandela Comprehensive High School, he prides himself on his success in transforming the school. He highlights three essential characteristics which led to his success: a stable personality, knowing one's responsibility, and an understanding of situations and needs. And yet despite his successes, his family had suffered as a consequence of his efforts and he cannot help wondering if there was something he could have done differently?

CASE STUDY SIX

BOOMTOWN DÉJÀ VU

Fanie Cloete

GHOSTS OF THE PAST

The time is 1997 and the place the new, post-apartheid Republic of South Africa. John Oliver puts his brand-new cellular phone back on his huge, gleaming desk and slumps forward with his head in his hands, smiling wryly. He feels totally frustrated and powerless. If he had suspected that he would receive a call like this, he would not have accepted his recent appointment as City Manager of Madlala.

Madlala is an over-crowded, mainly black, city on the fringe of a highly urbanised industrial area in Natal. Conditions in the city have become desperate: no municipal services are possible in some parts of the city, due to the continued political and faction fighting which had been aggravated by the formal declaration of the magisterial district as an unrest area two months ago. Conflict has simmered in this region of the country since the first free and democratic elections which founded the new state in April 1994. After a bloody massacre of 17 party guests one Saturday night in a city night-club, an incident rumoured to be politically motivated, the Provincial Government interceded, and sent the Provincial Guard into the area to attempt to restore law and order. Since then, the situation has deteriorated: some street blocks are now literally war zones and no-go areas for any side.

The telephone call Oliver has just received was from the Provincial Director-General of Local Government, who informed him that the Premier has decided to initiate a huge urban development project in the middle of "Bosnia" (as the core section of the conflict area is now known), to improve living conditions there. Of course, Oliver suspects that the real reason the Premier has decided to stick his nose into the mess is because he wants to mobilise support in the area for the coming local elections and he had hoped to get the backing of the local city council for his proposal.

Oliver's protestations – that the project was not feasible under current conditions – fell on deaf ears. The Premier apparently feels so strongly about the project that he is prepared to go ahead with it "in the interests of the region", even without the council's support.

Oliver's thoughts drifted back to his experiences in Boomtown in the mid eighties, when, as a senior project analyst at the Southern Regional Development

Agency (SOREDA), he had had to deal with the consequences of a problematic urban development programme. "This is going to be another Boomtown all over again. Just my bad luck!" he mumbled.

BOOMTOWN

Boomtown, a dormitory suburb near an important industrial area, comprised an area of 2,5 square kilometres where 200,000 people lived in desperate conditions. Some of the residents worked nearby in a fairly affluent white residential area or in other parts of the metropolitan area within easy reach. The township was strategically situated, near train and bus routes, and was therefore a popular settlement that experienced a rapid influx of people from outlying rural and peri-urban areas.

Although some original residents bought stands when the township was developed early this century and had good quality structures built, conditions in the township quickly deteriorated. This was due in part to the fast rate of urbanisation and the apartheid government's policy of slum clearance whereby minimum services and facilities were provided in order to induce urban migrants to locate elsewhere.

This slum clearance policy had been strenuously resisted by the black residents over the years. In fact, the township had a long history of intense political activism and tended to draw strong political leaders on the basis of this reputation. It was a hotbed of resistance against the government's policy of Separate Development, and for most of the mid eighties had been, almost continuously, a formally declared unrest area, under strict police and even military supervision and control.

Services and facilities in the township were minimal. Most houses or shacks had no electricity or running water; open pit sewerage systems were the norm, and refuse removal was infrequent. The township was one of the most densely populated areas in the country. Squatters had put up shacks on every available open space, including below the flood-line of the nearby river running through the metropolitan area and into one of the region's major irrigation dams in that region.

The township was boxed in on all sides by industrial and white residential areas, which meant it had no growth potential. The cumulative effect of these conditions presented serious overcrowding, pollution and health crises – not to mention a potential flood disaster.

An obvious need existed for urban renewal. Most residents, however, refused to move, even temporarily. In any case, there were no adjacent open spaces available.

THE COUNCIL AND THE PROJECT

The government's race policies led to the establishment of a black local authority in Boomtown. This development was fiercely resisted by the residents, but eventually forced on the community. A City Council had been established comprising government-nominated candidates, all of whom were unopposed in the first election, indicating that the Council was considered illegitimate and rejected by the community. Council members were isolated from the community, unable to hold public meetings for fear of violence. Most of them were continuously subject to harassment and frequent attacks on their lives and property, and requested permanent police protection.

Although the Council had wide powers, it did not have access to sufficient finances to enable it to improve the quality of life of Boomtown residents.

In mid 1986, the entire council resigned, some members voluntarily but most under pressure from the community. An administrator was appointed in terms of the legislation in operation in such areas at the time, while most of the former councillors were retained as an advisory committee to support the administrator in his decisions. The administrator was a capable if somewhat authoritarian person, and although he did not succeed in establishing full rapport with community leaders, he initially drew praise for improving community services through better management.

He quickly realised the ballooning parameters of the various crises in the Boomtown community, and requested financial assistance from the National Housing Fund for an urgent urban upgrading project, aimed at diminishing the health risks and generally improving conditions in the township. He had the support of most of the ex-councillors for an extensive electrification programme, the installation of water taps and ablution facilities at strategic locations, including centrally placed flush toilets, a water-borne sewerage system, the tarring of main routes through the community, and the construction of pavements and additional housing units. The estimated cost of the upgrading programme was R50 million. It was generally acknowledged that the scheme was long overdue and work needed to begin as soon as possible. However, for various reasons, it was not possible to get formal community approval or support for the proposed project.

CIVIC STRUCTURES

The community of Boomtown had become well organised and mobilised into various interest groups and organisations through its long history of fighting the government and its policies.

Three main civic organisations existed. They competed fiercely for the support of the Boomtown inhabitants, although few political differences existed among them. In fact, the leaders of the different organisations all professed to be active members of the dominant political party in the township. Their differences related mostly to personality conflicts or different strategies and tactics. They were:

The Boomtown Property Owners Association (BPOA)
This was the oldest but smallest of the three interest groups, representing the original established land owners. They consisted of the upper crust of Boom-

town society: the business and professional sectors. They were politically moderate and pragmatic. Many ex-councillors were leading figures in the BPOA, whose membership had declined over time. Its main competitor was the BRA.

The Boomtown Residents Association (BRA)

This organisation represented the Boomtown middle-class majority, consisting of tenants renting accommodation from the land owners or from the Council. They constituted tenants of brick-and-mortar structures as well as of tin shacks put up in the backyards of stands on which the brick structures were built. They were typically industrial, clerical and administrative workers. The BRA's competitors were both the BPOA and the BRO, which respectively competed for the support of its top and its bottom-income members.

The Boomtown Residents Organisation (BRO)

The BRO was the newcomer in Boomtown. It represented virtually all the new settlers living in the tin shacks in the community: the squatters. Its membership was growing very fast but at the same time constituted a very disorganised and volatile interest group whose "loyalties" to Boomtown were frequently questioned by the older residents, because many members retained strong links with rural areas and spent weekends and holidays "at home" in those areas. The BRO's strongest competitor for support was the BRA.

Competition among the civics was very strong and emotional. They refused to talk to each other, and even to attend the same meetings or be in the same room. The BPOA had mixed feelings about the Council, because of the involvement of many of its members in it. The BRA's and BRO's common enemies were the Council/Administrator which they rejected, in principle, as being unrepresentative and illegitimate along with the state security structure which co-ordinated the national state of emergency and monitored the activities of community leaders.

Despite their differences, all the civics strongly supported the principle of upgrading community services and facilities, the abolition of the separate black local authority and the integration of their community into nearby affluent white City. While the BPOA supported the Council Administrator's development proposal with some qualifications, the BRA and the BRO rejected it outright, on the grounds that it was too little too late, emanated from a politically discredited and illegitimate system, and was being forced on the Boomtown community without prior consultation or their participation.

THE GOVERNMENT

The central government under P W Botha was, in 1987, under increasing pressure from all quarters to change its race policies. One of the policy strategies which it pursued was to re-establish law and order in those communities where it had broken down (like Boomtown) through strong security force intervention. The second phase of the strategy was to implement massive socio-economic development programmes in those communities under the direction of a Joint Management Committee System (JMC), co-ordinated by the military.

The objective was to divert community attention from their preoccupation with political issues and to provide opportunities for the middle classes to aspire towards economic and social improvement: the so-called WHAM (Winning Hearts and Minds) strategy.

Boomtown was regarded by the government as the ideal model on which to test this policy. An all-out effort was made to ensure the success of the project. The Council-Administrator of Boomtown was an important and active member of the local JMC, and the project was devised in that forum with his co-operation. The eventual objective was to transform Boomtown into a model community which would set the necessary example for others.

The existence of a national state of emergency facilitated the imposition of law and order in the community, and made it easier for the security forces to physically remove "trouble-makers".

THE DEVELOPMENT AGENCY

SOREDA was, at the time, a rural development agency which depended on grants from the government for approximately 80% of its funds. The agency realised that, in order to survive, it had to change its focus from a rural to an urban orientation. Its policy-makers were looking to effect this shift in focus by investing in an appropriate project. It had some funds available, but had not yet decided whether it should begin with a "greenfields" or an urban renewal project.

The executive chairperson of SOREDA received a telephone call from the Cabinet minister responsible for providing development funds to the organisation who "requested" SOREDA to consider allocating bridging finance to the upgrading of Boomtown. The original upgrading project had been approved by the National Housing Fund, but the Fund's money ran out before it could be implemented. Although the Fund would have been allocated sufficient money by the government during the following financial year, the looming crises in Boomtown made it imperative that the project be implemented as soon as possible. The minister was urging SOREDA to become involved in this project.

SOREDA commissioned a feasibility study of the project and John Oliver himself wrote the major portion of the subsequent report; he remembered how proud he was of it. The study concluded that the existing state of emergency as well as the lack of participation from the community could jeopardise the project's success. The project was clearly doomed without at least the tacit support of the community at an early stage, whilst the state of emergency made it very difficult to implement any project, especially in a complex community such as Boomtown.

In addition, it was clear that central government and its security establishment both had hidden agendas of their own and SOREDA would be subject to their directives and dependent on their assistance to maintain law and order in Boomtown, if it were to become involved in the project. SOREDA could not afford to become involved in a project which may backfire on it. On the other hand, SOREDA felt that its involvement might improve its own negative image and that of the project in the eyes of the community, and might facilitate SOREDA's entry into the urban development market. It could not be denied that a crisis of major proportions was brewing in Boomtown, and that SOREDA was probably the only vehicle available at such short notice to try to defuse that crisis. If it refused involvement, and the Boomtown situation exploded, it could be subjected to severe criticism. The organisation was anxious to avoid antagonising the government who was the main source of its funding. Besides, the required R50 million investment in the project was small in proportion to the contributions SOREDA was accustomed to making to projects and represented a small portion of its annual budget.

SOREDA decided to take the plunge and to sponsor the Boomtown upgrading project to the tune of R50 million. It would use this opportunity to achieve speedy entry into the urban development market. Top management regarded the Boomtown development project as a crucial strategic exercise which had to succeed at all costs. Oliver grimaced as he reflected on what had happened in Boomtown. One of SOREDA's explicit requirements was that the Council-Administrator was to keep the community informed and to attempt to secure their participation in the project through all possible and affordable means.

Secondly, the major contractor would have to take responsibility for negotiating all aspects of the implementation of the project with the community, including entry of property, temporary removals, water and electricity cuts, closure of streets, etc. Unfortunately, the contractor concerned had never been involved in a contract requiring political experience and sensitivity.

Because SOREDA regarded itself as a traditional development-financing institution, it decided that it should not become directly involved in the project, but should act only in a supportive role, providing advice and technical know-how to the client (the council/administrator) and the contractor through a joint supervisory project team consisting of SOREDA staff from different sections within the organisation as well as representatives from the offices of the contractor and the council administrator. Oliver was SOREDA's chief representative on this team.

At its first planning meeting, the joint project team had to formulate the most suitable implementation strategy and the roles of the various participants. Oliver was requested to advise the team about what they should and should not do. One of the first questions raised was what the role of the security forces should be in the project, and what SOREDA's relationship with them should be. In the absence of a feasible alternative, it was decided to co-operate with them in order to implement the project and attempt to protect SOREDA's R50 million investment, albeit at the cost of community participation and legitimisation.

The results of this decision were mixed: some community improvements were grudgingly accepted in the longer term, while others which did not have the approval of the community were rejected outright and even sabotaged at huge additional cost to SOREDA. However, in general, the community was drawn together and mobilised against the developer. The defiant spirit that grew among community leaders made them independent and headstrong spokespersons for the residents. They demanded to be consulted as early as possible on the smallest aspects, and tried to scuttle any project that did not comply with those demands. Only one of the civic organisations was given a formal role in negotiating structure, which effectively gave them veto powers over decisions affecting the community. Oliver felt that this move had probably created more problems for future administrators than it had solved, because it had accorded an ambitious and unaccountable community elite a power out of proportion to their real mandate.

BACK TO THE FUTURE

His thoughts came back to the current proposed development in the area called Bosnia in the city of Madlala. Development projects hinging on political expediency possessed grave dangers, he felt. He wished that there was enough time to bring in a firm of credible consultants to provide a full analysis for presentation to the provincial structures and the premier's office. Factors such as pressure from the top, community leadership struggles and an unstable environment for programme and project development linked Boomtown and Bosnia in his mind. Would he have to watch the same pattern of events that took place ten years ago unfold again? Walking through the municipal garage to his car Oliver wondered if there was anything he could do to positively influence the outcome in Bosnia.

CASE STUDY SEVEN

AN AUTHORITARIAN APPROACH TO MANAGEMENT

Salim Latib

Pascal Khumalo had grown up in a small town in a largely rural region whose economy was based on agriculture. His parents were hard-working and devout, and subjected their children to severe discipline. As a boy, Khumalo did odd jobs to pay for his own clothes and school supplies. He was a typical product of a society that valued the work ethic: disciplined, conservative, industrious, and respectful of authority.

At the university, where he studied public administration, Khumalo was interested mainly in those aspects of his courses that he considered down-to-earth. He found theoretical and philosophical propositions boring, because he had difficulty in applying the abstract to practical matters.

Upon graduation, Khumalo got his first job in his own region as an assistant to the director of the Social Welfare Department in Simelani, a rural municipality comprising about 40,000 residents that was neither wealthy nor poor. Demands on the social welfare service were not great, and the problems facing the department staff of ten were readily taken care of. Khumalo won the respect of his director and co-workers by his conscientious work and reliability. When the director moved on after a year, Khumalo succeeded him in the post.

A year later Khumalo accepted an offer to direct a department in a large municipality containing more industry, a more varied economy, and a more diverse population than Simelani's. Khumalo became head of a department, with forty staff members, that was governed by the Naledi Social Service Commission. It was a typical public welfare agency, administered by the municipality, supervised by the regional government, and funded by the municipality, regional and central governments. Its programmes included Aid for Families with Dependent Children (AFDC), Work Incentive (WIN), Supplemental Security Income (SSI), and Medicaid, all administered under guidelines set by the regional and central governments.

The staff members, Khumalo soon discovered, frequently failed to follow the guidelines and even appeared unfamiliar with them, applied rules inconsistently, and were sometimes indifferent to their clients' needs. Employees often arrived late at the office; took time off to take care of personal matters without permission; left clients waiting while they drank coffee or chatted with fellow employees and, in general, were inefficient and lackadaisical. Khumalo found that few of them had the education and training for their work, and quickly discovered the reason: qualified people were hard to obtain because of the low pay scale, the minimum acceptable by regional government standards. The Naledi Social Service commissioners, who were all conservative politically and economically, held budgets to the lowest possible level. Consequently salary levels in all municipal offices were uncompetitive with those in the private sector.

Khumalo's initial review of the agency revealed that three people appeared potentially useful in establishing an organisational structure to replace the existing slipshod operation. They were the assistant director and two others, who had ill-defined supervisory powers.

The course of action to reform the agency appeared clear to Khumalo. What was needed was a highly structured and disciplined organisation. He envisioned himself as keeping a finger on all programmes administered by the agency. Supervisors would be selected from within the organisation. Authority would be delegated to them, and line workers would be classified according to a strict hierarchy. Jobs would be highly specialised and all employees would be trained to perform their duties in a prescribed manner. Weekly staff meetings would be used to review and modify work styles and to inculcate respect for authority.

In putting his plans into effect Khumalo rejected suggestions from the workers. He felt that their ideas on pay, job design, and office procedures had no place in a well-run operation. "If they don't like the way the office is run, they can work somewhere else", he said. Despite Khumalo's authoritarian approach to management, some improvements were beginning to show. The office was brightened by fresh paint and the furniture was rearranged so that counsellors had more privacy in discussing problems with their clients. Responsibility for certain tasks was assigned to specific people, files were kept up-to-date, and clients' requests were handled more quickly. Khumalo and his supervisors, carefully chosen from among the staff, seemed to receive proper respect from other employees.

But mounting dissatisfaction and dissent soon boiled over. Line workers challenged Khumalo's edicts at staff meetings, complained about many of the imposed rules and regulations, wrangled over policies and goals, and threatened to appeal to the governing boards. Khumalo's supervisors periodically approached him with suggestions for changes. Khumalo was upset and felt they were interfering with his prerogatives as an administrator. Yet he was willing to listen to their opinions, especially as he began to fear losing his job if the extent of the objections among the staff reached the agency's governing boards.

The supervisors explained to him that many improvements had been made in the department, but they believed the administrative structure had to be made more responsive to staff personnel. They suggested that staff input in salary plans, office-procedural policies, and staff meetings be increased and that a programme of upgrading jobs and pay be introduced. They felt that the new administrative system was possibly too strict, whereas under the former director the department had not been tightly controlled, the work had been done and the public had seemed satisfied with the level of service they received.

It was hard for Khumalo to accept that he had been wrong in thinking that the welfare department needed a more rigid structure, but he now recognised that his reform had failed and that there were aspects of management to which he had been blind.

QUESTIONS 1:

a) Analyse Khumalo's conception of leadership.
b) Drawing on appropriate theories of leadership, describe the style of leadership you think would be most appropriate for Khumalo to use in this situation.

QUESTION 2:

Suppose you have been asked by Khumalo to assist him in drawing up a training and development plan for the staff of his department when he is first appointed to the Naledi Social Services Department. Draw up a report for Khumalo which sets out recommendations, together with arguments to justify them.

QUESTION 3:

a) Analyse the assumptions regarding organisational design which lay behind the changes Khumalo brought into the Naledi Social Service Commission.
b) What alternative approaches to organisational theory would you recommend Khumalo should have considered? What might have been the consequences of his adopting the alternative you recommend?

QUESTION 4:

a) Design an appropriate performance appraisal system that could be used by Khumalo to determine the effectiveness and efficiency of individual staff members at the Naledi Social Service Commission.
b) Explain how he could use this system as part of a performance management approach to improve performance of his department.

QUESTION 5:

a) Analyse the organisational factors which impeded Khumalo's efforts to effect change in the Naledi Social Service Commission.
b) Explain how Khumalo could have managed blockages and resistance to change in the Naledi Social Services Department, and briefly outline a strategy for change that Khumalo could have implemented so as to be more successful.

QUESTION 6:

a) Analyse the motivational theories that are reflected in the changes that Khumalo initiated in the Naledi Social Service Commission.
b) Advise Khumalo on the different approaches to motivation in an organisation. In addition, detail, for Khumalo's use, a strategy for dealing with the motivational problems at the Naledi Social Service Commission.

CASE STUDY EIGHT

JOHANNESBURG HOSPITAL NURSING SERVICES

Jacqui Myburgh

WIFE TURNS NURSE IN HOSPITAL CRISIS

A city councillor was summoned urgently to the crisis-torn Johannesburg Hospital – to nurse her husband because no trained staff were available.

Mrs Patricia Lion-Cachet, National Party representative for the Hill and Regent's Park, also hired a private nurse as a 'body-guard' to ensure her husband's well-being while in hospital. Her husband, Rene, managing director of Shareworld, was admitted to the respiratory intensive care unit after being struck down by the disease Guillain Barre, which leaves the victim temporarily paralysed.

He spent four and a half months in the unit – and his wife was at his side every afternoon and every evening.

Horror

"It cost more than R10 000 for private nursing, but after all the stories we've heard, and our own experience, it was worth every cent," said Mrs Lion-Cachet this week.

"The nursing situation in that unit is so critical, families have to make their own arrangements to ensure their loved ones get the right treatment and correct medication.

"The final straw came when the hospital telephoned me in desperation one Sunday morning and asked me to come to the ICU because there were no staff.

"I know as little about ICU nursing as about driving a bus!"

While they have nothing but praise for the few full-time nurses in the unit, the Lion-Cachets said at times it was left in the hands of untrained nurse aides.

"What we saw there defies description. No wonder there are so many reports of patients being given the wrong medication," said Mr Lion-Cachet.

He saw the aides "shovelling food down trachea tubes" and said several patients whose bowels had to be cleared were left unattended for extended periods.

"Most of the people in that unit can't even speak and rely on the nursing staff for all their needs.

"If it wasn't so serious, it could even be amusing. Once, when I tried to signal to an agency nurse by smacking my lips that I was thirsty, she thought I was flirting and gave me a kiss."

Specialist treatment through which hostile antibodies are washed out of the blood enabled him to make what doctors have described as a "remarkable recovery".

But Mr Lion-Cachet is still haunted by the horror of his experience in the specialist unit.

He is just one of a growing band of former patients who have slammed their treatment at the hospital.

The ICU is designed to accommodate 24 patients, but the intake has been reduced to 4 due to lack of staff.

It is manned by agency nurses who are inexperienced or unqualified in ICU techniques and unfamiliar with the sophisticated life-giving equipment the patients rely on.

Mr Manuel Vianna, another Guillain Barre victim has been transferred to the neurological ward because there is no one to care for him in the ICU.

Critically ill, he recently choked and contracted pneumonia after food was forced into his trachea tube and went into his lungs by mistake.

The wife of an accountant who was hospitalised for a year after being hit by the syndrome said he had been left for almost two months on one occasion before his paralysed bowel was cleaned out.

"I encountered a lot of goodwill in that unit, but I believe my husband's health has suffered badly from what appears to me to be negligence by the hospital."

"When his bowel finally perforated, it happened on a Sunday, when only one operating theatre in the entire hospital was functioning.

"He nearly died while waiting for surgery," said the woman, who did not want to be named.

In addition, he contracted pneumonia three times, septicaemia and peritonitis while in hospital.

This week, Professor Jeremy Kallenbach, who resigned as head of the unit in protest against the "appalling" conditions, warned that it would have to close unless drastic steps were taken soon.

The acting superintendent of the hospital, Dr Trevor Frankish, refused to comment on claims of neglect but said that he would do "everything possible" to keep vital units functioning.

Figure 1: *Sunday Times Metro,* April 1, 1990

APRIL 2, 1990

Outside, it was a perfect autumn Monday on the highveld. But inside the Johannesburg Hospital, chaos reigned. Dr. Trevor Frankish replaced the telephone receiver with a sense of near panic. He had taken over the hospital as Acting Chief Superintendent just the day before, following the resignation of the Chief Superintendent. But, from the time he had walked into the office, the phone had not stopped ringing. The problem was the article in the previous day's *Sunday Times Metro* regarding the nursing treatment of a high-profile patient (see Figure 1).

The Director of Hospital Services in Pretoria was the first to call. He wanted a full report on the matter as soon as possible. Then three newspapers and two radio stations phoned to follow up the story. Television news wanted an interview with him before 16:00. The latest caller was the Minister of Health, who had phoned him directly for a report.

What to do? First, he called in Dr. Kalmyn, a very experienced Deputy Superintendent, and asked her to investigate the problems in the Intensive Care Unit as a matter of urgency. Then, Dr. Frankish felt that it was imperative for him to assess the nursing situation in the hospital generally. As a first step, he read the letter left by the outgoing Superintendent, which detailed his understanding of the nursing problem (see Appendix 1).

He then decided to convene a number of focus groups with registered nurses, nursing service managers, patients, doctors and superintendents, to try and identify the main problems as quickly as possible. He decided that he would ask the groups some general questions about why people chose nursing as a career, why they had chosen to work at the Johannesburg Hospital, its mission, what they thought about the structure and systems in nursing, how they evaluated the quality of service, what they thought the function of nurses was, what their expectations were, and where they thought the major problems lay.

WHAT THE NURSES SAID

The discussions with 20 registered nurses revealed some interesting facts. (See Appendix 2 for some background to the nursing profession in South Africa.) Dr Frankish discovered that there were various reasons that nurses chose nursing as a career. A common reason given was the motivation to care for people, but many had enrolled for nursing because they could get paid while training. Some nurses had initially applied to study medicine but were not accepted, so had then applied for nursing training, in the knowledge that there were always vacancies.

They had chosen to nurse specifically at the Johannesburg Hospital for a multiplicity of reasons:

"It is an academic hospital and we enjoy the stimulation of case discussion."

"It is an English hospital."

"The crèche is cheap."

"No posts were available at other hospitals."

"State benefits are good and there are a wide variety of in-house training courses of an extremely high standard."

However, there was universal unhappiness with the merit system of evaluation. Nurses have to collect "incidents" which show that they have performed well. They present these annually to their supervisor who writes a supporting motivation. The nurses generally had this to say about the merit system:

"We don't like to be the ones to pat ourselves on the back. Another problem is that after the evaluation it could take a year or more before we receive our bonuses. It would be much better if our nursing service manager could do the evaluation."

The reward system is limited to once-off bonuses and a 'promotability rating.' For example, a nurse who completes a nursing degree receives a once-off payment at the end of the five-year training, but her salary remains the same as that of diploma nurses. Many nurses felt that there should be automatic and permanent financial recognition for completing courses, such as trauma nursing, theatre and intensive care.

Most nurses felt that the structure of nursing was bad in that nurses reach their top salaries relatively quickly and are then obliged to go into nursing administration to improve their salaries. Many nurses said that they would prefer to stay at their patients' bedsides, but progress up the ranks meant moving further and further away from the patient into an administrative role. Most preferred the patient contact.

Salary was an important issue to all the nurses. One sister, who had 30 years of experience, said:

"After all these years my take-home pay is only R1 630,00!"

The nurses felt that the ceiling on salary levels should be removed so that years of experience would count.

"All I can do to improve my income is to moonlight but I don't like to do it because I do my normal job well and I'm very tired after a day's work. And often a day's work is 12 hours."

Most agreed that nurses leave the profession because of the salary levels. Those nurses who continued in nursing in spite of the salaries did so because of a "need to care".

"I left the Johannesburg Hospital after I had finished my training and had worked there for one year. I then went overseas and worked in England for five years, where I was eventually promoted to sister-in-charge of a paediatric ward. When I returned I was put in a junior sister's position because I had not had two years of uninterrupted service with the Johannesburg Hospital. My years of experience in England counted for nothing!"

The in-service training courses provided at the hospital were regarded as being of a very high standard. There was concern that the new, four year training course for nurses produced graduates who were too theoretical and were unable to manage on their own. Nevertheless, they felt that the training gave nurses a holistic view of the patient and that this was a good thing.

All nurses knew that the hospital had a mission statement, and where it could be found in each ward. Many said *"It's quite long, but I don't really know what it has to say."*

When asked how they evaluate and control the quality of their service, the nurses responded that this is done by:

- looking at the patient and noting his mental state: *"If he's cheerful things are probably OK"*;
- checking things such as drips and charts, temperatures, blood pressures, and water jugs: *"If these things have all been done well we think most other things will also be right"*;
- nursing service managers who inspect the wards, talk to patients and check charts, medicines, stocks and registers;
- the number of complaints received from patients. Complaints are directed to the superintendent and do not necessarily get back to the ward;
- informal feedback received from other departments in the hospital where a patient may have complained about or complimented the ward staff;
- length of stay in hospital;
- incidence of hospital-acquired infections. This is monitored by an efficient and effective infection control service. However, there is no on-going measurement: *"We are not really informed whether the incidence of infection is higher or lower than during the same period last year"*;
- the number of medico-legal claims against the hospital;
- the evaluation forms completed by patients. *"We give the forms to all patients just before they go home, but very few fill them in."*

The nurses were unanimous that the factor most seriously affecting their ability to provide a quality service was the inefficiency of the support services.

"We could cope with the nursing shortage much better if we didn't have to do everyone else's work as well. If a porter is delayed, the nurse must push the patient. If the physiotherapist doesn't come, the nurse is expected to do the physiotherapy. We are really just 'polyfilla' because we have to fill in for all other services. And the worst is the food which is always late and often cold."

"Our job is multi-faceted enough as it is without our having to do everyone else's work too. For example, we change the linen, ensure that the patient gets his food and gets all his tests done. We give all the prescribed treatment such as drugs and changing of dressings, make sure that the patient gets seen by the physiotherapists, the occupational therapists, the social workers and the doctors. We manage the ward's stock, the cleaning staff, the duties of the nursing staff, allocate shifts, train the student nurses, write reports .... if one of these things is not done we must either

get hold of the person responsible for doing it or do it ourselves."

Other factors affecting nursing were (in order of importance):

- the shortage of nurses;
- the high turnover of staff;
- the high level of care required by patients in the hospital.

The high turnover of staff was seen to be "normal" because *"There is always a high turnover in first jobs"*. Often people left nursing because they felt that they had made the wrong career choice. Both black and white staff were reported to have left because of racial problems in the hospital, particularly since the staff became integrated. Black staff felt that their cultural norms were not understood or respected.

"When a black person dies we all give money to the family. When I circulated a collection list to my black colleagues after a black patient died in one of the wards, I was reprimanded and I still have to face a disciplinary enquiry."

The nurses felt that the expectations of patients were generally met.

"Patients simply want to be treated like people. The greatest fears patients have is loss of independence and that they will be given the wrong treatment. Those who have been hospitalised previously expect at least the same level of care, but times have changed."

When questioned about what they feel doctors expect of nurses, the general feeling was:

"We feel that the doctors seem to expect nurses to clean up after them. They also expect nurses to give quality care to the patient, to keep them informed about the patient and at all times to be efficient. Interns are generally arrogant and need to be put in their place. Doctors and nurses need to trust each other more."

WHAT THE PATIENTS SAID

Discussions with a random sample of patients revealed the following comments:

"Last time I was treated at a private hospital and I would have chosen to go back there because I know the place. But because my treatment was being controlled through the Johannesburg Hospital, my GP said I should come here."

"No-one likes to go to a new club and even less a new hospital. Perhaps a sister could have talked to me during the first half-hour or so to make me feel at home."

"I was apprehensive when I came in. You read about people who have a leg cut off after going in with a sore ear. So I was worried that the wrong treatment might be given to me."

"The attention I got here, particularly from the white sisters, was very good. They obviously form the backbone of the industry. Most of the black nurses are also

excellent, they just do things differently. The nurses have really instilled confidence in me. In the open market you couldn't get this calibre of person for less than R6 000 per month. I asked a sister one day why she didn't go out and get a better paid job. She replied 'No, I'm dedicated to my job here'. It seems unfair to trade on dedication and pay low salaries."

"I know the quality of care here is good. If I wake up at night there is someone busy doing something for me. I don't think there's anything more that they could be doing for me."

"There is no panic in an emergency. They really know what they are doing."

"I must say that I find it unusual to hear doctors and student nurses speaking on first name terms. In the UK when you talk to a doctor you have to lift your hat."

"I feel nervous to complain too much, because I have seen some nurses ignore some of the patients who complain. They seem to gang up against the more difficult patients."

WHAT THE DOCTORS SAID

The doctors felt that the task of nurses was to ensure that all the investigations were done timeously and that the prescribed treatment was carried out effectively. Doctors claimed that minor omissions or mistakes (and occasionally a serious mistake) have occurred all too frequently in the treatment and monitoring of patients.

"It is not unusual to find that blood pressure recordings vary from one shift to the next and from those done by the doctor."

They attribute this to the heavy work load that nurses have to cope with and to a deterioration in standards especially among student nurses.

Medical interns voiced some disapproval of the way the nurses treated them and of the standard of nursing care.

"I am often called out at night for situations which are not really emergencies."

"My drips are often blocked. The intravenous fluids are not replaced timeously and the drips run dry."

The interns claimed that patients often complained to them about deficiencies. They would alert the ward sister who would try to do something about it. The medical interns felt that the nursing problem was caused mainly by low wages, which in turn resulted in many of the experienced nurses leaving.

WHAT THE NURSING SERVICE MANAGERS (MATRONS) SAID

Nursing service managers believed that some young people became nurses for "romantic" reasons. Either they were "looking for a husband amongst the eligible *young medical students"* or they had *"an outmoded concept of the nurse mopping the fevered brow."*

"When they have to confront reality and find that nursing is extremely hard work, both physically and intellectually, many leave nursing. In fact about 30% of student nurses leave in the first few months."

"Many nurses have been patients before, and the experience made them want to become nurses."

Some nursing service managers felt that the independence nursing training offered was an attraction to nursing. The provision of salary and accommodation during training was regarded as very appealing.

"Some of our students had tried office work but found it unsatisfying and switched to nursing."

"We feel that nurses choose to work at the Johannesburg Hospital for a variety of reasons. The hospital has a good name amongst the public."

"It is in a good location."

One nursing service manager who had trained at the hospital said:

"The hospital is painted in bright colours and that appealed to me. Other hospitals look so dull. Everything happens here, the hospital is alive."

Another major attraction of the Johannesburg Hospital is the B G Alexander Nursing College. It was the first nursing college in South Africa and has a reputation for providing excellent training courses. The prospect of doing a post-registration course at the College is also a draw-card to the hospital.

Nursing service managers agreed that the low salary was the main problem facing nursing.

"Many nurses are single parents and they need money to survive. The only way they can legally get more income is to do night duty or work in areas which have special allowances such as theatre or intensive care. Of course they can also moonlight but it is illegal."

Nursing service managers saw the effect of low salaries as the most serious problem facing nursing services. They also agreed with the nurses that the support services were a major problem area.

They were aware of the hospital mission statement and its contents but were under the impression that it *"was being revised at present"*. They stated that they were not involved in any discussions on the matter, nor had they asked whether they could make a contribution.

The nursing service managers measure quality by:

- regular and frequent inspection of nursing documents;
- ward inspections;

- daily ward rounds;
- stock control;
- statistics on rates of hospital-acquired infections.

The results of their inspections are fed back to the wards but they do not record their findings on charts for the wards. The nursing service managers were concerned that a lot of information about patients captured on the hospital computer was getting lost. They felt that statistics could be beneficial to them, and that it would help to measure and control quality of care.

They felt that people see nurses from four points of view: from the patients' point of view they are *"treasures"*; from the young man's point of view they are *"tarts"*; from a feminist's point of view that are *"slaves"* and from the media's point of view they are *"tyrants"*.

"It is just not the revered profession it used to be, particularly in South Africa. Women no longer see it as a career option."

Nursing service managers thought patients most feared getting lost and forgotten in a large hospital. There was acknowledgement that patients generally fear reprisal should they complain.

"The doctors only want nurses to be obedient. They want slaves! And the surgeons are the worst!"

"They also expect us to be experts, but they don't like their decisions challenged!"

When questioned about racial integration at the hospital, one nursing service manager had this to say:

"Since the hospital became racially integrated cultural issues have created problems. For example black patients do not feel they should tell the doctor what is wrong with them. It is for the doctor to tell them what is wrong. These cultural issues need to be identified and understood. There are patients from many diverse language and cultural groups here. There are often many Portuguese and Italian patients as well as black South Africans speaking a wide range of African languages. In fact, translation has become a major function that nurses have to perform, particularly the black nurses."

Nursing service managers felt that the hospital could be made more attractive to nurses if:
- it were widely communicated that, because of the shift system, working hours are very flexible and that the hospital makes an effort to accommodate nurses;
- more listed courses were developed, such as, for example, a course in advanced medical nursing;
- the status of nursing as a profession was improved.

"Nurses tend to develop a fierce loyalty to their training hospital and great care must be taken not to disparage other hospitals".

WHAT THE MEDICAL SUPERINTENDENTS SAID

The medical superintendents saw nurses largely as idealists who are prepared to provide a service which is both physically and emotionally demanding, despite low pay. They felt that some nurses had chosen to nurse at the Johannesburg General Hospital because of the geographic location of the hospital relative to the next nearest provincial hospital and because of the modern facilities available. Student pay and the need to care were also factors which they identified.

They believed that the most important problem facing nursing was the low pay issue, which was beyond the chief superintendent's sphere of influence. Other problems they identified were the inflexibility of nursing management and the hospital bureaucracy. They also felt that one of the greatest problems was the poor communication in the hospital.

"There is no effective formal channel of communication between nursing staff and management except in certain areas of the hospital."

The superintendents identified labour relations as being the major obstacle to the smooth running of support services. Labour relations are handled centrally and hospital personnel have not, until now, been able to talk to the unions directly.

"Major problems are experienced every pay-day. Staff leave their posts to get their cheques and then disappear to the bank to get their money. They don't come back at all that day and the services collapse."

The superintendents were asked what could be done to make a patient "delighted" with his stay in hospital. Dr. Kalmyn said:

"Many of the outcomes are very sad and it is not realistic to expect patients to be 'delighted'. The best we should hope for is to get the patients to feel 'grateful' or perhaps 'happy' but not 'delighted'. But to achieve that, a great number of staff would be required to not only treat patients, but to talk to them as well."

The mission statement of the hospital was discussed. The superintendents stated that they wanted to revise the mission statement. They had recently inserted the mission statement into the hospital newsletter *Contact* inviting comment from the 6 000 staff. Only three replies were forthcoming. They were looking for a slogan or concise statement which would be relevant and all staff could "buy into".

DR KALMYN'S REPORT-BACK ON THE ICU CRISIS

"The Respiratory Intensive Care Unit has been going through a particularly difficult phase. Qualified intensive care nursing personnel are simply not available to work in the unit despite the fact that the unit is a very closely-knit team headed by Prof. Jeremy Kallenbach. Unfortunately the incidence of critically ill cases has been escalating recently and the unit has been running six beds instead of four. Most nurses

in the hospital refuse to work there because they are completely intimidated by the high-technology machines. Intensive care nursing requires highly skilled and well-trained nurses.

"Many nurses who were compelled to work in the unit resigned. As a result the nursing service manager made use of agency nurses when they were available. Sometimes agency nurses did not turn up and the exhausted day staff simply could not continue."

MR AND MRS LION-CACHET'S SIDE OF THE STORY

Mrs Lion-Cachet had the highest praise for the permanent nursing staff in the unit but held the hospital responsible for providing adequate levels of staffing. She felt that the use of agency nurses was a medico-legal hazard.

She stated that the article in the Sunday Times Metro was grossly exaggerated. She had not seen nurse aides *"shovelling food down trachea tubes"* as stated in the article, but had indeed been asked to come and assist in the unit by an agency nurse-aide whilst the sister in charge had been dealing with an emergency. She felt, however, that the reasons were sound.

"Family members are far more concerned about the welfare of a relative than any nurse aide would be. Competent family members are sometimes called upon when there are staff shortages in the unit. They assist with very basic nursing and observation of the patient."

WHAT TO DO?

Dr Trevor Frankish felt that he had achieved a fair understanding of the nursing situation at the hospital. It was evident that there were some areas in which nursing services broke down completely at times, particularly at night in the general wards, but also occasionally in the specialised units like the Intensive Care Unit. It appeared that the acute problem in the ICU was a symptom of a deeper and more fundamental nursing problem at the hospital. He weighed up his options:

He could tell the media that an enquiry had been launched and that a full report would be made to the Director of Hospital Services whom the media could contact in about a week (or some other deliberately vague target date). This would give him time to strategise.

OR

He could extract all the correspondence with the Director over the last six months or so relating to the nursing shortages at the hospital and point out that the hospital had previously warned that the pressures on it were such that incidents of this nature could be expected. In this way he could pass the buck up the line and keep himself out of trouble.

OR

He could investigate the entire nursing service in the hospital, identify all correctable factors, and come up with some solutions. He would have to admit to the media (and head office) that there were correctable problems which had given rise to the incident and that he would do his best to ensure that such an incident did not recur.

"But," he thought, *"it would be sad to see the Johannesburg Hospital's reputation damaged by this incident."*

He wondered if there was a way to turn this failure of service to the hospital's advantage.

APPENDIX 1

EXTRACTS FROM THE OUTGOING SUPERINTENDENT'S LETTER

1. THE JOHANNESBURG HOSPITAL – BACKGROUND

The hospital was established in 1890 as a successor to a small hospital in the Johannesburg Jail. It was a prestigious building for its time and has remained a major factor in the life of the City of Johannesburg since its inception.

In 1919, the Medical Faculty of the University of the Witwatersrand was founded and the Hospital has been associated with the University as its main teaching hospital ever since.

The Hospital moved from Hillbrow to its current site in Parktown in 1979. It was built as the flagship hospital of the Transvaal Provincial Administration's hospital services. It was to have 2 000 beds and was to provide all the training facilities required by the Faculty of Medicine.

As a provincial hospital, it was intended that it should supply services to the poor (indigent patients). Its location in Parktown, one of the wealthiest suburbs in South Africa, is particularly inappropriate for its intended patient population. Neither the staff nor the patients come from this area.

The new hospital has never had more than 1 150 of its 2 000 beds in use and is currently battling to service some 800 beds. Initially, the inability to open all the beds in the hospital was due to the scarcity of nursing staff (of whom the hospital currently employs about 2 000) but later, as black staff became available (i.e. politically acceptable), the State began to experience a major financial crisis and funds dried up. There were no funds to employ additional nurses or provide any additional medical services. Although there were a large number of unemployed nurses, the Hospital remained in a state of permanent crisis due to nursing shortages.

The hospital has a staff of nearly 6 000 people, of which about 600 are doctors. It provides a full range of medical services (with the exception of cardiac transplantation) and treats about 600 000 out-patients annually.

Until 1990, it functioned both as a community hospital, admitting all indigent white patients in its area, and as a referral hospital, to which complicated cases (which could not be adequately managed at other provincial or private hospitals) were referred. Today, although the Hospital is legally open to all population groups, the persistent shortage of funds and staff has prevented a major racial shift in the patient population.

2. NURSING SERVICES

Modern hospital medicine is totally dependent on the presence of adequately trained nursing staff. Without adequate numbers of nurses, doctors cannot be utilised to their fullest extent and available therapies may have to be withheld from patients. Indeed, positively dangerous situations may develop, in which patients' lives are in danger.

A number of factors external to the hospital have influenced the quality and quantity of nursing staff. Some of these are outlined as follows:

2.1 Nursing Training

Problem 1: The new nursing training course

Up to 1987, nursing training consisted of a three year training course provided by a nursing college, under the auspices of the Hospital. However, in 1989, the Nursing Council announced that there would be a new nursing training course of four years duration. This was to be an integrated course which would include three former postgraduate courses (Midwifery, Psychiatric Nursing and Community Health Nursing). By eliminating duplication in the various training course syllabi, this would allow nurses qualifying through this course to emerge qualified in General Nursing, Midwifery, Psychiatric Nursing and Community Health Nursing.

Prior to the four-year course, about 20% of nurses who qualified in the general three-year course went on to train in midwifery, 10% in psychiatry and 5% in community health nursing. Each of these courses had required an additional year of training and nurses who had passed these courses were regarded by both medical and nursing colleagues as being sufficiently well trained to be able to take responsibility in their field of specialisation.

Problem 2: Night duty cover

The Nursing Council also announced that student nurses (on whom the training hospitals relied) were allowed to do only one third of the night duty that they had been doing, and that night duty areas would be dictated by training needs as determined by principals of newly independent training colleges, and not by the hospital nursing services.

Problem 3: Funds

To make matters worse, hospitals were informed that no additional funds were available for staff to perform the student nurse function and they were to cope as best they could.

Problem 4: Break in supply of qualified staff

The change from a three-year to a four-year course means that in three years' time there will be a year in which no new nurses qualify so hospitals would have to survive a period without a new intake of trained staff.

Problem 5: Hopelessly inadequate training facilities

Since all student nurses now require training in midwifery instead of the previous 20%, the average birth-rate at the hospital is totally inadequate for their training needs. Therefore student nurses have to be sent away from the training hospitals to far corners of the province to find the necessary patients. This development further depleted the nursing personnel at the hospital.

The situation is even worse as far as training for psychiatric nursing and for community nursing are concerned. However, this has had no impact on the hospital.

Problem 6: The University of the Witwatersrand

The University of the Witwatersrand, like many other universities, provides a degree course in nursing. However, few, if any, of the graduate nurses ever return to bedside nursing.

2.2 Nursing as a Profession

South African hospitals have been experiencing a severe shortage of nursing staff in common with most Western countries for some time. The shortage is so severe that many of the senior medical staff, in their personal capacities, have been paying nurses in their units to work overtime in order to maintain high standards of care.

Although private hospitals have made use of nurses from all population groups, no Provincial (now State) hospitals have been allowed to do so. This has been an extremely sensitive political issue, as the "authorities" have not wanted to be seen to steal nurses from the black population to assist the whites.

There seemed to be a general feeling that whites had to take care of their own health needs. After a long struggle, this hospital was permitted to employ a small quota of black nurses, provided they were not employed in another provincial hospital. This meant that the most sophisticated hospital in the province had to select from those nurses who, by and large, were not the most able. This fact did not facilitate the introduction of a non-racial nursing service. The fact that black nurses did not qualify either for accommodation in the hospital residences or for crèche facilities aggravated the situation. They were not even allowed onto the municipal buses (the only public transport to the hospital).

As business and other career opportunities have opened up to white women, so fewer and fewer wish to train as nurses. The Johannesburg Hospital's nursing college battled to fill its 200 posts each year (while Baragwanath Hospital had to sift through some 4 000 to 6 000 applications). Those who did enter nursing were often unsuitable and were just trying nursing for lack of an alternative.

2.3 Use of Nurses by the State

The state attempted to reduce the costs of medical care by keeping nursing salaries low. This has become increasingly effective in deterring competent matriculants from choosing nursing as a career.

The new four-year training course was intended to make nursing a more professional service, the training being similar in length to the study period for an honours degree. Unfortunately, the State has made no provision for increasing the salaries of nurses who complete the four-year course so that the extended duration without any appropriate incentive dissuades many prospective nurses, who are, in any case, more practically than academically orientated, from entering nursing.

3. MEDICAL SERVICES

The medical staff consists of trainees (interns and registrars) and consultants who teach and provide specialist services. The quality of medical care at the hospital has always been of the highest order. As a result, competent, dedicated doctors have competed for posts at the hospital. However, this is no longer uniformly true and some specialist services have been terminated, while others have been drastically curtailed.

The Commission for Administration, which is responsible for determining salaries of all classes of State employees, does not pay market-related salaries. Many of these highly dedicated doctors are forced to leave the hospital as their family commitments grow, and to enter private practice.

The salary lag became increasingly evident during the 1980s, with the result that certain crucial departments (for example, radiology) had no hope of ever recruiting a full-time department head.

As the nursing crisis worsened, doctors were unable to implement therapies for lack of nursing staff. There were insufficient nurses to monitor patients on ventilators, and transplantation services were drastically curtailed. A professor refused to work in his intensive care unit, which he had run for over ten years, because he could not take responsibility for patients with his inadequate nursing staff. Many senior clinicians consulted their legal defence societies regarding their liability in the event of a mishap. Many have also written to the press or to politicians. The Medical Advisory Committee made representations to me and to the Provincial authorities. I myself, have been in regular communication with the State Attorney regarding the liability of the State and with my own legal defence society regarding my personal liability.

As operating theatre nursing staff dwindled, surgeons of all disciplines had their operating time reduced. No elective procedures could be performed as there was no time even to handle all the emergencies. Patients were being referred to other hospitals on a daily basis.

To aggravate the crisis, the economy of the country is in recession. The number of patients presenting for treatment has increased and the hospital is obliged to admit them even though nursing staff is inadequate for their needs. Complaints from patients have become a regular feature in the newspapers.

3.1 Academic Medicine

The University of the Witwatersrand uses five academic hospitals with a total of nearly 5 000 beds. The Faculty of Medicine requires only 2 000 beds for teaching purposes but, because of the failure of the State to provide services to Soweto and to black people living in Johannesburg, the University has taken on more and more service commitments.

It has become increasingly difficult for the faculty to provide comprehensive services to all of the academic hospitals. In an attempt to alleviate the situation, some services have been merged and racially integrated but others continue to decline to crisis levels. Proposals for amalgamation of some of the hospitals have been developed and presented to the State for consideration, but no action has yet been taken.

The Johannesburg Hospital is the newest hospital of the group and was initially well equipped. It is closely integrated with the new Medical Faculty buildings and is close to the library, laboratory and lecture theatres. This close relationship has caused jealousy amongst the group of hospitals and has made co-operation between hospitals seem impossible.

3.2 Structure of Hospital Services

Hospitals are graded in the following way:
- Community Hospitals, to serve a local community. These hospitals are run by medical officers (general practitioners) with part-time specialists in various disciplines.
- Regional Hospitals, to serve the local community and also to take referral cases from the surrounding community hospitals.
- Academic Hospitals, to serve the local community, to take referral patients and to provide super-specialist services such as transplantation, cancer therapy, neurosurgery, etc.

This structure forces the Johannesburg Hospital to admit all indigent patients who present here, which causes tremendous overload on the available resources. Doctors use all means at their disposal to have patients transferred to other hospitals (this includes reliance on racial, geographic or financial classification). The hospital management has repeatedly asked for "closed hospital" status which would permit it to take only serious emergencies directly, while all other patients would have to be "referred in" from a regional hospital. Such a system would allow the hospital management to control the load on each department and to keep within the allocated budget. Apparently this has been regarded as a radical suggestion and the State has not accepted it. The University has also opposed the proposal, as their teaching philosophy requires that each teaching hospital should offer a reasonable mix of patients.

APPENDIX 2a

BACKGROUND TO THE NURSING PROFESSION IN SOUTH AFRICA

STATUTORY ORGANISATIONS

The South African Nursing Council (SANC)

The SANC is a public body, responsible to, and established for the protection of, the public. The council controls and regulates nursing training and teaching, acts as the disciplinarian of the nursing profession and ensures that regulations are obeyed. It keeps a register and a roll of all nurses in the country. In order to practise, a nurse must be registered with the SANC.

The South African Nursing Association (SANA)

SANA is the national representative body concerned with the organisation of the professional, and was established mainly to further the interests of nurses. All categories and races of nurses are required by law to join the SANA (Vlok, 1988: 73,77).

APPENDIX 2b

THE NURSE PRACTIONER

A practitioner of nursing is the professionally trained and registered nurse, who is legally empowered by the Nursing Act, No. 50 of 1978, to carry joint responsibility with the doctor for patient care, and who is fully accountable for her own acts and omissions.

The law empowers the nurse to practise her profession in any type of healthcare situation. The parameters of the profession include independent decision-making, collaboration, facilitation, advocacy, nursing diagnosis, planning of nursing care and recording of actions on behalf of the patient (Vlok, 1988: 47).

Categories of Nurses

The nursing profession is graded into four levels, according to qualifications as defined by the SANC:

Registered Nurses (RN): have undergone a three or the new four-year diploma in general nursing, or the five-year degree course. The minimum entry requirement is a matric pass. Since the advent of the new four-year diploma, all registered nurses qualify as general nurse, midwife, psychiatric nurse and community health nurse. Registered nurses who have completed the three-year diploma course may further their training by specialising in one or more of 31 disciplines.

Enrolled Nurses (EN): also called Staff Nurses, have undergone a two-year training period, and have at least a Standard Eight pass.

Enrolled Nursing Assistants (ENA): have undergone a training of at least one hundred days. They must be in possession of at least a Standard Six pass.

Student and Pupil Nurses: a person who is training to become a Registered Nurse or an Enrolled Nurse respectively.

Distribution of SANA members according to nursing category
(SANC Statistical Returns, 1990)

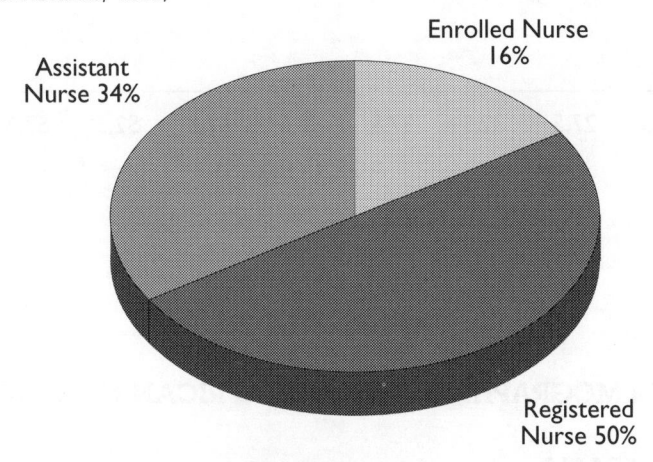

- Enrolled Nurse 16%
- Assistant Nurse 34%
- Registered Nurse 50%

APPENDIX 2c

REMUNERATION OF NURSES

"Salary is the single most important factor causing the nurse shortage. Nurses' salaries lag very far behind those of comparably qualified and experienced staff in both the public and private sectors" (Dewar in Myburgh, 1990: 159).

At the annual conference held In February 1990, SANA recommended that nurses' salaries be increased by 60%, thus raising the starting salary of a newly qualified Registered Nurse from R15 000 to R25 000 per annum. Later in 1990, the Government increased the salaries of nurses by 20–40%, depending on experience and length of service.

The following graph shows the comparison of median salaries between the nursing sector and the rest of the public sector:

COMPARISON OF MEDIAN SALARIES

According to age, between the Nursing Sector and the rest of the Public Sector

RANDS PER YEAR (THOUSANDS)

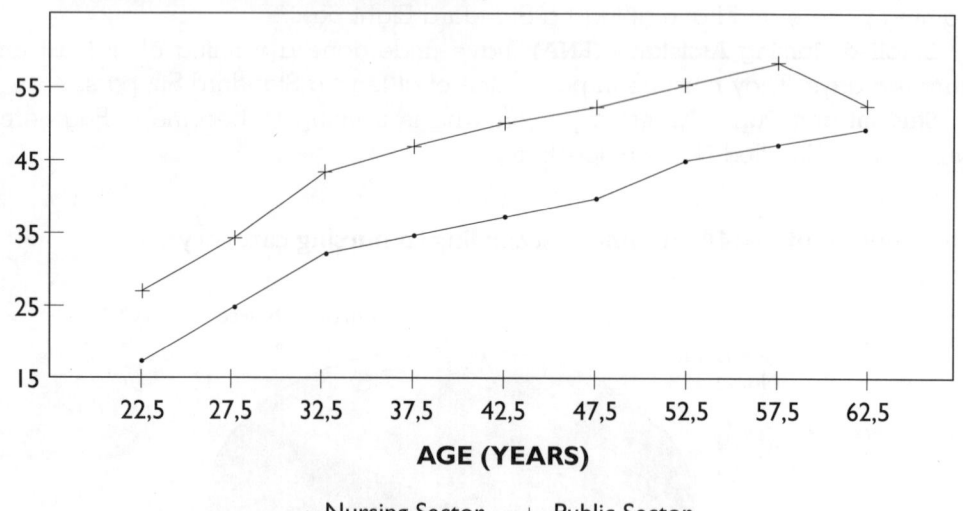

— Nursing Sector   + Public Sector

APPENDIX 2d

DEMOGRAPHICS OF SOUTH AFRICAN NURSING

Membership of SANA

As at 19 February 1991, there were 144 325 practising nurses in South Africa (including former TVBC states). The following pie-chart shows the distribution of SANA members according to population group.

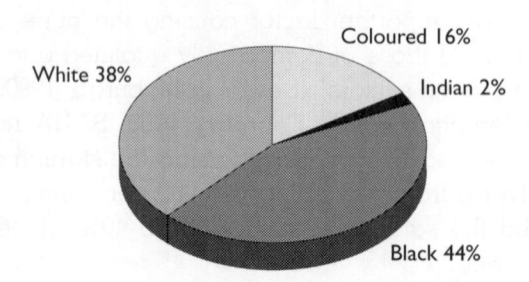

White 38%
Coloured 16%
Indian 2%
Black 44%

Nurses as a percentage of the total health-care personnel

The following chart shows that nurses form 55% of the total health-care force, demonstrating the crucial role they play in maintaining the nation's health.

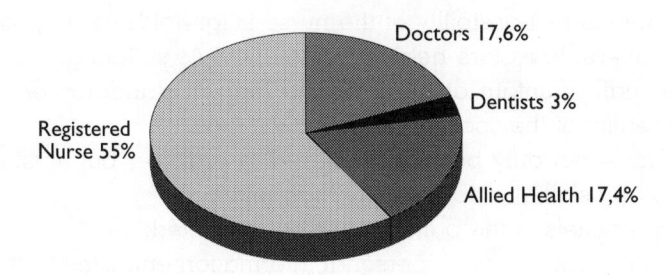

- Doctors 17,6%
- Dentists 3%
- Allied Health 17,4%
- Registered Nurse 55%

Category distribution of Nurses according to population group
(SANC Statistical Returns, 1990)

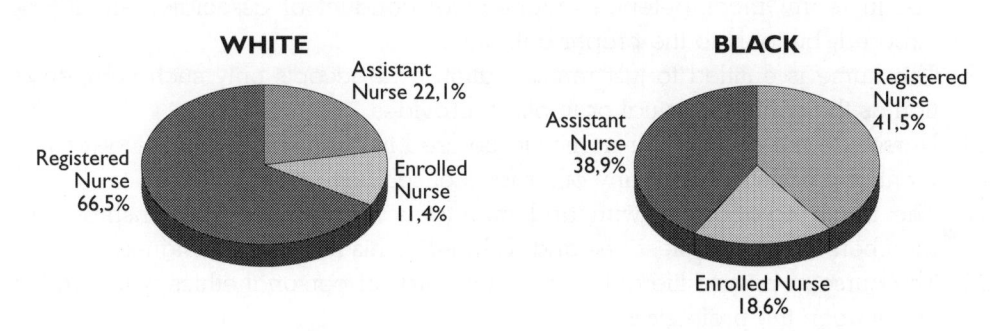

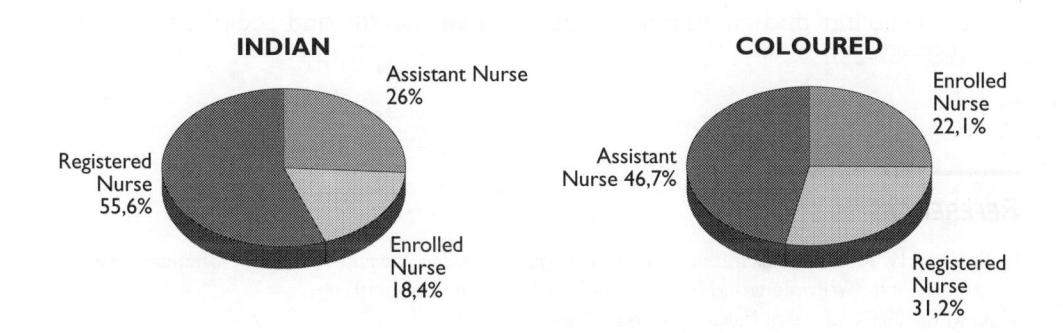

WHITE
- Registered Nurse 66,5%
- Assistant Nurse 22,1%
- Enrolled Nurse 11,4%

BLACK
- Registered Nurse 41,5%
- Assistant Nurse 38,9%
- Enrolled Nurse 18,6%

INDIAN
- Registered Nurse 55,6%
- Assistant Nurse 26%
- Enrolled Nurse 18,4%

COLOURED
- Enrolled Nurse 22,1%
- Assistant Nurse 46,7%
- Registered Nurse 31,2%

APPENDIX 2e

THE INTERNATIONAL COUNCIL OF NURSES (ICN) CODE OF NURSING ETHICS

1. The fundamental responsibility of the nurse is fourfold: viz. to promote health, to prevent illness, to restore health and to alleviate suffering.
2. The nurse shall maintain at all times the highest standards of care possible within the reality of the specific situation.
3. The nurse must not only be well prepared to practise, but must maintain her knowledge and skill at a consistently high level.
4. The religious beliefs of the patient must be respected.
5. Nurses hold in confidence all personal information entrusted to them.
6. The nurse must recognise not only responsibility, but the limitations of her or his professional functions.
7. The nurse sustains a co-operative relationship with co-workers in nursing and other fields.
8. The nurse sustains confidence in the physician and other members of the health team; incompetence or unethical conduct of associates should be exposed, but only to the proper authority.
9. The nurse is entitled to just remuneration and accepts only such compensation as the contract, actual or implied, provides.
10. Nurses do not permit their names to be used in connection with the advertisement of products or with any other form of self advertisement.
11. The nurse co-operates with and maintains harmonious relationships with members of other professions and with her or his nursing colleagues.
12. The nurse in private life adheres to standards of personal ethics which reflect credit upon the profession.
13. In personal conduct, nurses should not knowingly disregard the accepted patterns of behaviour of the community in which they live and work.
14. The nurse should participate in and share with other citizens the responsibility for initiating and supporting action to meet health and social needs (Vlok, 1988: 57–59).

REFERENCES

Myburgh, J H. 1990. *Unionism and Collective Bargaining in the Nursing Profession.* Johannesburg: University of the Witwatersrand (unpublished MBA Research Report)

Vlok, M E. 1988. *Manual of Nursing.* 9th ed. Cape Town: Juta

CASE STUDY NINE

ACADEMIC MANAGEMENT AND MANAGING ACADEMICS

William Fox

Prof. Johan van der Spuy, Chairperson of the Department of Public and Development Management at the University of Stellen-West, is on his way across campus to attend a Senate meeting, having attended a Board meeting of the Faculty of Economic and Management Sciences. He cannot understand why the board could not have met on a day other than that of the Senate. As a result of the Dean's leniency in letting the chairperson of Statistics waste the gathering's time on petty issues, he would now be late for his next meeting.

Johan has a very important matter on his mind which he would have liked to discuss with the Dean, Derrick McDonald, but there was no time during or after the Faculty Board meeting to do so. Derrick himself is a busy man, running from one meeting to another, and Johan has not been able to discuss the matter with him in detail, although they have had a telephonic conversation in which the problem was at least defined. However, it was a solution Johan needed, but it seemed that further discussion with Derrick would have to wait until Monday.

DECISIONS AND PROBLEMS

The meeting of Senate is well underway by the time Johan enters the room. The Principal, Kobus Hartzhorn, stops in the middle of a sentence ... "Welcome Prof. Van der Spuy – better late than never." On looking around, Johan cannot see any of his faculty colleagues present, not even Derrick. In view of the consequential decision faced by the Senate regarding the establishment of a School of Government in neighbouring Transmibia, in co-operation with the State University of Transmibia, Johan would have thought it important that faculty members affected be present to raise the many questions and concerns that had been circulating in the department. He had not had sufficient time to go through all of the reports, but had many reservations about the advisability of the University's committing a large slice of its resources to this one project

Transmibia is an emerging state and a valued neighbour. Its University has good standing internationally, and the decision to establish the School had been taken by the political leaders of the two countries. Johan was concerned that the decision had been taken too hastily, without proper consideration of the capacity needed to ensure success. His department was already stretched to the limit as far as lecturing and student counselling were concerned, and he doubted whether they would be able to cope with the additional workload.

"How far have we gone with the agenda?" Johan asks the colleague seated next to him, Peter Hauptfleisch from Botany.

"We are still discussing the parking problem at the Science building. I wish they could find a solution, because I'm considering staying at home, except on days when I hold lectures, if they don't do something about it," Peter whispers, indifferent to whoever is listening.

Johan is fairly satisfied with his own parking arrangements on campus, so his thoughts wander off to his own most pressing problem: Joan Sullivan. Joan was one of his best lecturers, and an excellent researcher. She has been with the Department for 19 years, and had it not been for blatant discrimination, she could have been more than an Associate Professor by now. Johan starts to trace in his mind the events which have led to the present crisis in his department. About two years ago Joan went through a painful divorce. At that stage everyone within the department commented on how well she had adapted to her circumstances. Joan had always suffered mild insomnia and had regularly taken prescribed drugs to help her cope. However, after her divorce, she had taken heavier and heavier dosages, and within six months she was experiencing problems related to mild addiction.

When she was not promoted to a full professorship 18 months ago, despite the strong recommendations by the Department as a whole, her drug-taking got out of hand. Complaints were received from students and colleagues that Joan tended to deliver outdated lectures or was sporadically absent. Her research had deteriorated to the point where she was entirely unproductive, and he had felt obliged to have a serious discussion with her.

Three months ago, Joan had failed to show up for lectures on two consecutive days. After repeated telephone calls went unanswered, he decided to visit her apartment in the company of Pat Smythe. The caretaker had let them into the apartment, which they found to be in total chaos. Joan was in such a bad state that he had had to call an ambulance. At the hospital, the medical officer confirmed that Joan had a serious drug problem. After her release from hospital, Johan once again had a serious discussion with Joan, and matters seemed to improve for a week or two. Then the cycle of events was repeated. He had suggested to Joan that she attend a rehabilitation clinic, but she had been adamant that she could rehabilitate herself. She had assured Johan that her personal life was at last settling down.

"Does Prof. Van der Spuy wish to comment?" With a shock Johan realises that Kobus is addressing the question to him.

"I'm sorry, Chair, I did not quite get the question."

"We were having a discussion on the merits of having permanent parking facilities available on Campus, and were wondering whether your Department would have any objections," came the sarcastic reply.

"No objections, although we ourselves do not have any problems."

"So, then, we are decided: permanent parking at a fixed monthly rate for all professors on Campus, and rotational parking for all other personnel."

Let it go, Johan decides. My colleagues won't like it, but I cannot make a further fool of myself by trying to reopen discussions. As he is thinking this, Kobus announces that they have now spent half an hour on the issue of parking and that their time limit of three hours for a Senate meeting is in danger of being exceeded if they do not move on at a more rapid pace.

"The next item on the agenda, which is the establishment of a School of Government in Transmibia, is now open for discussion. Prof. Van der Spuy, as your Department will be closely involved, do you have any comments?"

"Yes, Chair, I wish to put it to Senate that, in the opinion of my Department, the lack of resources makes this a very risky undertaking for the University as a whole. If ..."

"Let me remind you, Prof. Van der Spuy, that the principle of the matter was decided by Council early this year. The resolution was made on the recommendation of the Academic Planning Committee, of which your Dean is a member."

"I realise that, Chair, but that does not mean that we have to move on the matter at this particular stage."

"Time is running out. At least two other universities are interested, and the necessary funds have been voted by Council. We cannot afford any delay!"

"May I then, Chair, enquire what assistance my Department can expect when the new School becomes operative?" "As you know, Prof. Van der Spuy, Senate does not discuss matters related to finances; that is a matter for the Executive Committee of Council. Do you wish to discuss the contents of the programmes your Department has prepared?"

"No, Chair, we are satisfied with their contents."

"So, let us move on then: any further comments?"

As Johan resumes his seat, Peter whispers, "You should have known that the Council resolution was final."

"Yes, but they did not put a date to it!"

"You had that pressing staff matter to attend to during the last meeting of Senate. During the tea break Kobus informed us that nothing was going to stop his establishing the School in Transmibia before the end of this year."

"I didn't know that, otherwise I would have kept my big mouth shut."

On his way back to his office Johan reflects on the curious way in which Senate makes decisions. Parking matters take up half an hour of its time, while a matter of international, national and institutional importance takes five minutes to decide. He is still not sure that his Department will be able to cope, but they will have to do their level best.

JOAN – A HASTY DECISION

When Johan reaches his office, he sees a big brown envelope, addressed to him personally and marked "Strictly Confidential", lying on his desk. On opening the envelope he reads from the copy sent to him by Kobus of the letter addressed to Joan:

12 October

Prof. Joan D Sullivan
Department of Public and Development Management
University of Stellen-West

Dear Prof. Sullivan

It is with great regret that I have to address this letter to you. I hoped that things could have been otherwise, but I have been left with no alternative.

The Chair of your Department has informed me on a number of occasions that, during the past few months, you have been unable to cope with your lecturing and research programmes. Furthermore, students have reported that you have repeatedly appeared in classes in a dazed state and were not able to handle the lecture at all. The personnel of both local and public government offices which you have visited recently in connection with your current research project have reported that you have caused disruptions and have been abusive to a point where, on at least one occasion, you had to be removed from the premises.

The parents of many students have also complained and indicated that their children do not seem to be making any progress at the Department, and, finally, some of your colleagues have complained that your behaviour of late has been disruptive and bad for morale.

In the circumstances I am of the opinion that you have the following options:

1. You immediately avail yourself of the leave owing to your credit and attend a rehabilitation centre.

2. You discuss with the Director of Personnel a severance package and related matters.

3. You retire with immediate effect, but your official retirement commences on conclusion of any period of leave you may have to your credit.

4. You delay the matter and risk disciplinary action being taken against you.

The University management realises that you have served the institution loyally for close on 20 years. However, your condition has caused a disruptive atmosphere within the Department, and this can no longer be tolerated.

You are welcome to discuss any decision you make with me personally before making it known to the authorities.

Finally, I would like to convey my best wishes to you for a bright and productive future.

Sincerely yours

(Prof.) Derrick McDonald
DEAN

cc Kobus Hartzhorn

Johan is stunned. How could Derrick do such a thing without knowing all the details or consulting with him? In any case, if Joan decided to seek legal advice, the University could be in big trouble. What would such a letter do to Joan? Although he does not want to contemplate it, he knows that she could do something drastic.

A telephone call to Derrick's office confirms that he has left for the weekend. There is also no reply from his home telephone. Johan realises that Derrick has left for his holiday cottage at the sea. The only thing to do is to travel there now. He hopes that Joan has not yet received the letter.

While driving to Derrick's cottage, Johan reflects on the way his management role in an academic environment has been developing. He has to admit to himself that he has a growing feeling that life is running away with him. He is no longer able to plan his time properly, which affects his ability to manage well and to make considered decisions. Certain matters being decided over his head, without his input and participation, are an increasing source of frustration. Today has been a perfect example of this problem, he thinks to himself. He is beginning to have serious doubts about the appropriateness of the management culture prevalent at the university. Surely there must be more effective management styles and techniques and much better ways of developing management capacity and skills amongst academics?

CASE STUDY TEN

CAREERISTS AND POLITICAL APPOINTEES IN THE PUBLIC SERVICE: CONFLICTS IN POLICY IMPLEMENTATION

Msizi Fakude

"I really do not know what Dube is up to. Since he joined us ten months ago, I have painstakingly gone through the whole policy implementation process with him. I have shown him how we go about recruiting personnel, trained him in our selection procedures, helped him to master our training methods and finally taught him all about our department's career development programme. In fact, I have imparted to him all he needs to know to implement our Affirmative Action Development Programme."

Perplexity was written all over Kobus Dreyer's face as he continued: "Surely, Sir, you won't find a more efficient and conscientious mentor than I have been to Sipho Dube!"

Dr Albie Meiring, the Director of Human Resources Management for the South City Council, half listened to his deputy's monologue as he glanced at the memorandum that Dreyer had placed before him. He was not surprised by the problem facing him now. The Director had anticipated such misunderstandings in his department since the newly elected South City Council had directed it to "formulate and implement employment policies in line with the changing political environment". Mr Dube had been appointed in terms of the new policy, and Mr Meiring had expected some initial trouble.

A MEMORANDUM OF COMPLAINTS

When Dreyer had left his office, Meiring turned his attention to the memorandum that had been left with him:

MEMORANDUM

TO: Dr Albie Meiring, Director Human Resources Management
FROM: Mr Kobus Dreyer, Deputy Director Human Resources Management
RE: Mr Sipho Dube, Assistant Director Human Resources Development

I wish to lodge a complaint against Mr Sipho Dube's actions in our task of implementing the Affirmative Action Policy as directed by the South City Council.

Detailed evidence in support of my complaint is listed below:

1. Mr Dube continually questions and seeks to redefine the department's accepted procedures and criteria for the recruitment and selection of personnel under our new Affirmative Action Programme as laid down in the council's Policy Implementation Guidelines.

2. Mr Dube tends to apply what I consider to be overtly political criteria in his interviews of applicants. His interviews are peppered with questions about the interviewee's "experience with civic associations", "community involvement", "view of a future civil service" and "commitment to change". I feel strongly that such questions are irrelevant in the council.

3. Mr Dube continually voices his dissatisfaction with the efficiency of our policy formulation processes and policy implementation procedures. This is evident in his blatant disregard for the content and practices of our training programmes. Instead Mr Dube has, against the council's regulations, sought to supplement or even replace some of the content with what he calls an "empowering and developmental curriculum".

Our programme, according to the council's guidelines, is supposed to be a long-term process of socialisation of new applicants into the council's organisational culture. But Mr Dube seems to be keen on short-term and visible goals. He has thus wasted little time in seeing to it that new recruits carry out the changes that he deems to be urgent and essential.

In conclusion, I think Mr Dube's actions are detrimental to efficient and proper implementation of our task; and counter-productive and in conflict with the public service ethos. This makes it difficult for me, as his superior, to supervise and evaluate his performance.

I am concerned about being held accountable for the outcome of Mr Dube's implementation of the council's policies.

Meiring saw these complaints in the context of changes occurring on the political front. Over the past two years he had been aware of new and unnerving philosophies creeping into discussions, debates and papers at Public Service workshops. Why, even the old and respected *Publico*, the journal on local government, recently published a paper: "Towards a Responsible, Representative and Development Oriented Civil Service in South Africa", that he and his colleagues found disturbing. Meiring reflected sadly on the decrease in the number of articles and papers providing valuable, practical advice and guidelines on the implementation of new rules and regulations in local government.

Meiring sat brooding over the policy conflicts now besetting his department – just two years before his retirement. For over twenty years he and his deputy, having graduated from the North University with degrees in Public Administration, had diligently served various local governments. Many would say that few bureaucrats could match Kobus Dreyer or Dr Albie Meiring in experience, responsibility, equanimity and efficiency. But the changing political environment and the election of a new council for the South City, with its emphasis on client-related administration, accountability and representation, has presented his department with interesting but disturbing challenges.

SIPHO DUBE

Sipho Dube was aware that a formal complaint had been lodged against him, but was not really concerned as he knew he was occupying the moral high ground. He had the council's mandate to bring about substantive changes in the ethos of the administration. Sipho saw his actions as politically correct and necessary to achieve the desired institutional changes.

But the 30-year-old graduate from the new Graduate School of Public and Development Management had faced open hostility, criticism and obstruction to his work since joining the council ten months ago. His previous experience was limited to six years with the local civic association and he knew that his superiors did not really consider this valid experience. His Assistant-Deputy status also did not give him the necessary clout to effect the changes he knew were necessary. He wondered how the Director would react to his interpretation of the council's directives for the implementation of its Affirmative Action Development Programme. He began to fear that the Director would not, after all, see things his way, and decided to pay him a visit to give his side of the story.

WHAT TO DO?

Meiring sat back in his chair and tried to record the challenges facing him, reasoning that a list would make it all seem more manageable:

CHALLENGES
- How to reconcile the conflicting demands of maintaining a responsible and efficient administration within the standard rules and regulations laid down for local government and achieving public accountability, representation and client-centred administration, as directed by the new council.
- How to resolve, in a harmonious and fruitful way, the conflict between his deputy, Kobus Dreyer, and the new assistant, Sipho Dube.

EXERCISE:

You are Dr Albie Meiring, Director: Human Resources Management, South City Council. In light of the representation made to you by your Deputy, Mr Kobus Dreyer and by the Assistant Deputy Director, Mr Sipho Dube:
1. Identify the divergent interests on which Dreyer's and Dube's practices are premised;
2. Arrive at a solution satisfactory to Dube, Dreyer and the department as a whole and justify your solution on the grounds of its functionality;
3. Lay down appropriate ethical guidelines for the conduct of career civil servants towards political appointees and vice versa;
4. Determine what inclusions in the Local Government Code of Ethics are needed to serve the public interest;
5. Draft mechanisms for the solution of conflict between careerists and political appointees.

CASE STUDY ELEVEN

THE CASE OF ZIMETCO

Merle Favis

THE BIRTH OF AN NGO

In the wake of the massive demobilisation of liberation armies that took place at the conclusion of the lengthy war in Zimbabwe, a co-operative movement sprang up and thrived.

A number of individuals associated with production co-operatives in the Matabele Province, some of whom, as co-operative members, had received training at the Cody Institute of Canada, got together to discuss the need for education and training support for co-operatives in the region. They decided that the establishment of a new NGO might be the best way to tackle such a project and resolved to put the proposal to a range of co-operatives. Feedback was positive. Those canvassed felt that the initiative could fill a potentially serious shortfall in the development needs of the co-operative movement. They seemed particularly happy with the fact that the initiators were prominent and respected former combatants whose record of commitment to the movement was proven.

So it was that the Zimbabwe Education and Training Co-operative Collective, (Zimetco) was established in Matabele Province in 1981.

One of the collective's first steps was to establish a Management Committee. Members were drawn from, *inter alia*, church and educational backgrounds. Most were close associates of the founders; in fact, some had strong, long-standing personal or political ties with them. They were largely well-known and respected individuals within their community, and had considerable experience in organisational and development work.

Although the new Management Committee advertised available posts publicly, it was tacitly understood that staff would be drawn from the group of founders; they were, after all, "insiders" with the requisite understanding of the conditions facing Zimetco's target group.

The Management Committee set about planning Zimetco's programme, and a fund-raising drive was launched. At the time, Zimbabwe enjoyed a high international profile and, with northern NGOs and donor governments rallying to establish a presence in the newly independent state, funding was relatively easy to come by. Within a fairly short space of time Zimetco was up and running.

THE DEVELOPMENT OF ZIMETCO

During the first three years of its existence, Zimetco grew rapidly to become a successful and viable operation. The network of co-operatives in the region drew extensively on the services of the NGO, whose trainers organised central group workshops, and follow-up sessions with individual co-operatives, on a regular basis. Zimetco's staff understood training needs in this field and their timely response, effectively stimulated further demand. In the early days a forum comprising client co-operatives met regularly to give direction to Zimetco, but, with the NGOs growth in size and sophistication, this forum eventually disappeared.

In time, Zimetco linked up with a number of similar NGOs based in other parts of the country, through informal exchange of information. In 1984, the need to facilitate joint materials development and training workshops for co-operative members and trainees prompted this loose network of country-wide training NGOs to form themselves into an association: the Zimbabwe Co-operative Support Association (ZICSA).

To enable Zimetco to keep up with the demand for its services, an additional six members of staff, including administration and training personnel, were recruited from among the ranks of the co-operative movement. New staff members were thoroughly inducted and integrated into the organisation.

The successful development of Zimetco was largely facilitated by its Co-ordinator, Eli Mdou, a man of great dynamism and vision, who inspired trust amongst his staff. The Management Committee had every confidence in Mdou, to the extent that they were quite happy to leave to him the responsibility for devising and implementing systems of proper management and control over key functions such as finance and staff performance. Mdou was a good communicator. He automatically and regularly reported back to the Committee on these issues, so that members did not consider it necessary to create special systems and written procedures to govern these functions.

When, in 1985, Mdou tendered his resignation from Zimetco to take up a post at the UNDP, the Management Committee was anxious to recruit someone of similar calibre to head up the organisation. As no existing staff member was considered suitable for the position, the Management Committee advertised the post widely.

Zimetco's recruitment campaign did not, however, throw up any obvious candidate. After much deliberation the Management Committee appointed William Urungu, a Kenyan whose experience lay in the co-ordination of a literacy network in Kenya. No-one on the Management Committee knew Urungu personally because he was a non-Zimbabwean, but his CV, references and performance at his interview had impressed the selection committee.

From the outset, it was clear that Urungu's style of leadership and management differed from that of his predecessor. He worked very hard, but kept to himself and did not communicate very comfortably with his colleagues. When he joined the organisation it was involved in an intensive training programme, and much of his time was devoted to facilitating and co-ordinating this process. The

Management Committee felt that they should give him some breathing space and not demand too much from him too soon, particularly given the fact that he was a foreigner who had to do much adjusting to local conditions.

THINGS FALL APART

In March 1986 the Co-operative Association, ZICSA, hosted an important national policy conference, funded by a northern donor agency, to which 200 people from all over Zimbabwe were invited. Because ZICSA had not yet established its own administrative infrastructure, Zimetco, as a key member agency of ZICSA, was given the task of administering the conference funds. For this role, Zimetco was accountable to a co-ordinating committee comprising various ZICSA-linked organisations whose responsibility it was to oversee the planning and implementation of all aspects of the conference.

The conference went off according to plan. However, some time later the co-operative movement was shaken by chance events. Zimetco's administrator, in seeking catering for a private family function, approached the company which had been awarded the catering contract for the ZICSA conference three months previously. Jovially, the catering consultant asked whether she, like Zimetco, would insist on a 30% discount on the company's standard rate. This surprised the administrator, who was also responsible for processing the organisation's accounts, as she did not recall the receipt of a discount on the catering contract. When she returned to the office she checked the financial records relating to the conference.

Sure enough, the budget, invoice and expenditure statements all corresponded; if there had been a 30% discount, there was no mention of it. The administrator decided to approach a member of the Management Committee on the matter. From there the issue was taken to the Committee itself.

At first the Committee was reluctant to act. It stretched their credulity to think that anyone in their organisation might have been involved in the misappropriation of funds. There was a lot at stake and the complaint was, after all, based on hearsay. An investigation could undermine morale and confidence in the organisation and in the co-ordinator, who was already regarded with scepticism given that he had come from a different organisational culture. On the other hand, if the matter were not investigated, the administrator would be unhappy and she would be likely to make known her suspicions to other members of staff. Zimetco would then find itself in deep crisis.

Under these circumstances the Management Committee decided to undertake a discreet inquiry. During the two weeks it took to follow up the matter, rumours began to circulate to the effect that the co-ordinator had been involved in fraudulent activities. Under the weight of speculation not only did Zimetco enter into a state of turbulence and uncertainty, but so did ZICSA, since the rumours related to mismanagement of its funds.

AN INQUIRY

The results of the Management Committee's investigation indicated that a formal and open enquiry was indeed required. During this time, tension between the various stakeholders had increased dramatically. Questions were raised about the "joint control" of ZICSA's funds which had been administered by Zimetco and ZICSA members were at pains to dissociate themselves from the rumours, fearing that donors would suspect, at best, the existence of bad financial management systems in their own organisations; Zimetco's Management Committee was attacked for slack monitoring and control procedures; its administrator was blamed for negligence, and so on. All in all, a great deal of blaming and defending was going on, with groups of individuals aligning themselves according to their perceived interests.

THE VERDICT

A formal inquiry found Urungu guilty of defrauding Zimetco by accepting a bribe in the form of a 30% discount to contract caterers. Despite the embarrassment experienced by both Zimetco and ZICSA as a result of reporting the crime to the police, both organisations agreed that, as a long term "investment" it had been the correct course of action. When the crisis had subsided, they focused their energies on rebuilding their slightly bruised organisations.

QUESTIONS

1. What went wrong in Zimetco/ZICSA which resulted in the misuse of funds?
2. What mechanisms could have been put in place to avoid the occurrence?
3. Who was a) responsible; b) liable; and c) accountable for the problem and why?

CASE STUDY TWELVE

GOING FOR LOVE, MONEY, POWER, POLITICS OR PRINCIPLES

Fanie Cloete

PART ONE: THE BOREDOM OF TEACHING

After five years of teaching different aspects of Governmental Studies at university, Frank Human was frustrated. During the preceding years he had had the opportunity to teach students at all levels, from undergraduates, to honours and masters levels students. Furthermore, he was on the verge of completing his doctoral studies and felt on top of his chosen field of speciality, which was ethnic conflict resolution.

He realised that the intellectual challenges originally posed by his academic and research interests had faded. He was frankly bored with teaching only the theoretical principles of government and wanted to explore new professional possibilities which would allow him to apply the knowledge and expertise which he felt he had accumulated over these years.

It was just four years since the Soweto riots of 1976 had been suppressed by the National Party government in South Africa. National politics were still in turmoil. Everybody was looking for possible ways out of a political crisis, which seemed to become more intractable by the day.

Frank had followed a conscious policy of striving for political independence by avoiding involvement in party politics. He had always argued that association with one political group would compromise his academic objectivity. But he was so frustrated with his life at that moment that he decided to waive this principle in the interests of trying to do something more socially relevant, even if it meant associating with one or other political group.

THE CHALLENGE OF POLICY MAKING

One of Frank's interests was policy analysis, which he taught both at undergraduate and graduate levels. He decided that he would like to try his hand at influencing government policy making in those directions that he felt would present better opportunities for resolution of some of the political problems facing his country.

One day he saw an advertisement in the local paper, advertising positions within a new governmental unit which had been created to advise the government on future political policies. The unit was only an institutional think-tank with no executive responsibilities for the implementation of policies. Although he differed in many respects from government policies, he decided to apply for a position in the unit reasoning that he wanted to see for himself how policies were really made and whether it was possible to influence those policies from inside an organisation like the national government. He planned to return to the academic world after a stint of three or four years in such a policy-making position. He began his new job at the beginning of 1981.

THE CONSTRAINTS OF POLICY MAKING

In his new position, Frank had to come to terms with three major new constraints. The first was his job description. He was required to research, conceive and plan the details of new constitutional policies for the government within the parameters of official macro-government policy, and to advise the government on what to do, how to do it and what the implications are of different courses of action. He was therefore required to plan new policies within the framework of existing policies – a task he decided was impossible. Given his reasons for accepting the job in the first place, this was also personally and politically unacceptable to him, as he interpreted his mandate as the expansion of the parameters of government policy.

The second constraint followed from the first: he realised that although he occupied a position as an official in the public service, his work would be highly political. He needed to be cautious in his attempts to expand government policy to its limits, as he would, more than likely, run the risk of antagonising the very people he wanted to persuade to listen to him. It was a situation which called for very delicate handling. He realised that in this process he might sometimes tread a politically dangerous path, but felt that strategies could be devised to minimise the risks.

The third constraint which he experienced was the generally accepted responsibility of a public official not to criticise government policy but to defend it in public even if he did not agree with it. Initially this was difficult to live with, but, as compensation, the job did allow him to personally advise government decision makers about what he thought they should or should not do in certain cases.

THE FRUSTRATIONS OF POLICY MAKING

Five years later, Frank was promoted to head the unit. His experiences in that time had been mixed. In some cases he had succeeded in changing government policies; in others he failed to influence policy in the direction he thought best.

He became convinced that political decision makers were reforming their policies too slowly, and that the process needed to be accelerated. There was, however, increasing political resistance to change from his more conservative colleagues and politicians.

In 1985 (four years after he started his new career in government), Frank received an attractive offer to return to academic life. He considered it seriously because it fitted in with his original career plan but found himself in the midst of an important and exciting project. After careful consideration and discussion with his colleagues, superiors, friends and family, he declined the offer.

Major factors in his decision were his relative satisfaction with his progress (especially with some major policy projects which he had concluded); the prospect of pursuing his personal objectives successfully; and the fringe benefits of such a senior policy position in government (both financial and in terms of the strategic influence of the position. His decision was in spite of the fact that he was becoming increasingly perturbed by the slow pace of change; the tremendous effort it took to persuade decision-makers of the necessity for certain decisions and actions; and the fact that he could not publicly criticise some policies which he had tried very hard, so far without success, to change. His frustrations were aggravated by the national state of emergency which was declared, just before he received the offer.

Ultimately, Frank felt that he could contribute constructively to further changes in government policies and that he should bear the frustrations of his job. He consoled himself with the argument that, were he to resign, he would probably be replaced by a more conservative person: growing resistance encountered from decision makers was accompanied by an increasingly conservative political atmosphere. By staying on he felt he could block advisors who might try to slow down change even more.

Meanwhile, the political climate in the country deteriorated rapidly. Political violence escalated and security strategists gradually became more influential at political level, as community activists were jailed and killed and political resistance groups were increasingly banned by the government. Frank disagreed with these strategies which he perceived to be aimed at political containment instead of addressing the real causes of the violence. The pace of his work and the inputs he tried to make to accelerate the pace of reform, slowed down significantly.

STRATEGIC OPTIONS

This development increasingly caused Frank to wonder whether he should not have accepted the offer to return to university eighteen months earlier. He again decided to stay on, but to use every opportunity he got to more aggressively promote his strong views about what should be done.

His position as government planner enabled him to voice his views in key policy documents and at crucial discussion forums inside and outside government where future political strategies were discussed and where direct access to political decision makers could be obtained. He was supported in this decision by a few colleagues and some politicians, including his Minister, who shared his views and concerns. The Minister allowed his senior officials large degrees of autonomy, and Frank was of the opinion that he used them as proxies to put forward views which he, in his own strategic personal and political interests, preferred not to do himself.

Frank decided to use this autonomy and all the legal and official influence which he could bring to bear to the full, to still try to influence selected crucial government policies into what he thought was the right direction. As a result of this decision, he found himself in increasing conflict with more colleagues and politicians, (especially in the security profession) about issues which were defined at the time as "security related".

A decision about his personal life then also influenced his situation. Early in 1987 (now 6 years after he entered government service), he married a woman who was actively involved in an activist organisation which opposed the government's political policies. Before the marriage he considered the possibility that this could be detrimental to his career, but love won through in the end. During a routine interview by a security official to renew his security clearance in 1988 he was not asked about his wife and did not volunteer any information about her when he was asked at the end of the interview whether he wanted to mention "anything else which the intelligence authorities should know". His maximum clearance was renewed, allowing him continued access to top level classified documents and information.

A few months later, however, Frank received information that intelligence officials were monitoring the activities of his wife. He immediately contacted and reassured his counterpart in the Intelligence Service that he would not contravene security laws by divulging any sensitive information to which he was privy. He invited his colleague to verify this undertaking by means of the normal intelligence-gathering capacity which his organisation had. Frank, however, made it clear that he was not prepared to ask her to resign from the organisation concerned because it operated fully within the law as a legal organisation. He also immediately briefed his superiors fully about the incident and about his views on the matter. They undertook to take the issue up with their respective colleagues and report back to him if necessary.

In the mean time Frank continued to argue strongly for accelerated changes in the country both in government and in opposition policies. In this process he became more and more outspoken about what he believed should be done. He did not hear anything more about his wife and assumed that the storm in the teacup (as he regarded it) had passed.

THE FINAL STRAW

Later during 1988, Frank went on an overseas trip. Immediately on his return he was called in by his superiors and notified that he was to be transferred to another position with equal rank to the one he had. He was told several days later that his security clearance had been withdrawn by security forces under the authority of another department. No reason for these actions were given, other than a comment that "you should know why". A final decision about his future would be taken later. He was, however, also informed that if his wife should resign from the anti-government organisation of which she was a member, it would facilitate the outcome of such a decision. Frank refused in principle to discuss his wife's position any further with them. He accepted these developments as interim actions and awaited the final outcome.

Frank was given a new title, office and a secretary and some routine matters to attend to. After three weeks he still had access to all the highly classified documents in his possession. He sorted them out himself and initiated their removal for safe keeping. Nothing further happened. He occupied himself by following up a few personal research interests which he had not previously had the time to pursue.

Six months later his situation was still largely the same. He still could not succeed in obtaining more information about the reasons for his transfer and loss of security clearance. The press got hold of the story about two weeks after Frank was informed of what was going to happen to him. Speculation was rife that it was done because of his wife's activities and/or "he had talked to the ANC", which was illegal at the time. Frank increasingly suspected political motives behind everything, especially when his minister was, uncharacteristically, unavailable for two weeks when he wanted to discuss the issue with him and then denied any knowledge about what had happened and why it had happened. He was told that the minister was powerless to do anything about the case because the actions against Frank were taken by officials in another department. At a later stage, the minister concerned did publicly support him, but then became embroiled in a political power struggle with some of his colleagues in Cabinet, and eventually lost much influence.

Both from Frank's, and from his department's side, it was clear that this situation could not continue. The matter had to be resolved in some way or another.

PART 2: REVISITING THE PAST

Part 1 of the case ends at a point where Frank Human and/or his department had to take one or more very crucial decisions.

After 6 months' virtual isolation in his department and being given nothing of real importance to do while no further action was taken against him, Frank Human decided to initiate action. He had ample opportunity to consider his options. After discarding other alternatives, he wrote a letter to his responsible minister, explaining what had happened and summarising his views on the whole matter. He then outlined three possible courses of action :

(a) that he be re-instated in his previous position: he argued that since no further action has been taken against him, he assumed that no proof was available that he had contravened any statute or policy. He, however, also explicitly assumed in his letter that this option was probably not feasible in the light of recent media reports about a fierce political power struggle between his minister and other colleagues in Cabinet. These reports indicated an ongoing inside struggle for political influence. Although he did not mention it, Frank suspected that some of the major players in this power game to be behind the strategy to withdraw his security clearance. It was inconceivable that his clearance would be re-issued to him in view of the prevailing political and security cultures at the time, as well as his consistent outspokenness about radical changes which were needed in prevailing government policies, and his refusal to try to persuade his wife to resign from her activist organisation.

(b) His second option was that he be brought to court or that a formal departmental enquiry be held about the whole affair. Frank also assumed explicitly that this option would probably not be feasible because the rules applicable to such enquiries required that all the relevant facts be made available to him in order to prepare for the proceedings. He assumed that this would not be politically feasible in the light of what had already transpired.

(c) His third option was to request "early retirement", provided for by section 15(5) of the Public Service Act 1984. This section provides for an official to be paid a monthly pension based on the basis of his length of service in government at that time.

Three weeks later Frank was notified that his request was granted. Two months later he became a civil pensioner at the age of 39 years, while his minister's shock resignation and retirement from politics took effect a month earlier. Frank decided not to pursue events any further. He eventually returned to academic life, but at a financial loss. Eight months after he left (on 2 February 1990), some major policy changes which he had promoted were accepted as part of official government policy. Frank felt vindicated, *inter alia* because of the positive reception which he received among his counterparts involved in the political freedom struggle, where his legitimacy suddenly rose to new heights.

Late one afternoon, soon after the new post-apartheid government came to power in 1994, Frank was approached out of the blue by one of his former counterparts who now was a senior official in the new reconstructed Department of Provincial Affairs. He was invited to join that department in a position very similar to the one which he relinquished 5 years earlier, but now at a higher rank and, of course, a higher salary linked to very attractive fringe benefits. The position had to be filled urgently, and permission was obtained from the new Public Service Commission to dispense with the normal recruitment formalities.

Frank felt as if he were reliving his past. The offer was seductive, because of the importance of the work which was exactly in his line of expertise, and because of the improved financial status which accompanied it. Frank had also by now acquired a taste for the high flow of adrenalin which invariably accompanies that job. Unfortunately an important consideration complicated his decision. He felt once bitten, twice shy. He felt somewhat wary of again becoming involved with an interest group whose policies he did not fully agree with, and who might try to impose their political ideology on him.

Frank must reply early the next morning. He knows that he will probably not sleep much that night.

CASE STUDY THIRTEEN

MOLEFE'S MAZE

Patrick Kelly

POINT ONE:
MOLEFE'S DILEMMA

Molefe Khuele was faced with a dilemma. He had been working in the Human Resources ministry for just over a year, where he was responsible for a unit that was examining ways of making the ministry more responsive to the needs of labour and the business community. He was well qualified for the job, as he had previously been an assistant secretary-general in one of the larger COSATU trade unions. His entry into the civil service had been achieved through his participation in the National Economic Forum, where he had impressed all parties with his understanding of human resource needs and of the interests that motivated different positions that were discussed. He had shown himself to be a hard worker, whether he was representing workers or sitting on a NEF technical committee, and would often stay on after most people had gone home, to finish work that he had been allocated. After the election in 1994, he had been approached with an offer by the Director-General of the Human Resources ministry, and he had accepted the position without hesitation. He felt that many things would change now that there was a democratic government and he wanted to be a catalyst of that change.

Molefe had, so far, enjoyed his time in the department and, although there had been some obstacles, he had learnt many things about the civil service and human resource issues. The role of his unit of five people was to network with unions and business organisations, glean their concerns and feed them back to the department. The legitimacy of the ministry had improved during this time but it was sometimes hard to get people in other Directorates to use initiative or to be creative in their dealings with the public. There wasn't much blatant corruption happening, but people just didn't put any great effort into their work. Molefe had discussed these concerns with his superior, Mr Joubert, but as yet nothing had happened. Now, a few months later, his director had told him that an inter-ministerial committee was being established that was going to draw up a code of conduct for the civil service. As the Human Resources ministry dealt with issues of people and work, they had been invited to send a representative and the Director-General suggested Molefe. Mr Joubert told him that if he accepted this assignment he would need to reduce his current responsibilities by about sixty percent; the project was expected to last for about six months. The organisers needed to know by the end of work that day whether he would be part of the team or not.

During that day Molefe turned the issues over in his mind. If he agreed to go it would be beneficial for his career and he might get to know a bit more about other parts of the civil service. He also felt that a code of conduct would be a useful tool to get people to work in a more enthusiastic and committed manner. On the other hand, his work was really beginning to take off and he felt that he was beginning to have some influence within other directorates. He believed that he could try to broaden the scope of his unit to look at effectiveness and innovation as well as responsiveness within the department.

> If you think he agreed to work on the committee,
> go to POINT TWO;
> if you think that he declined,
> go to POINT FOUR.

POINT TWO:
WORKS ON COMMITTEE

Molefe was apprehensive but excited as he took his seat in the conference room in the Civil Service Commission (CSC) building. Looking around the table he saw a mix of people from the old civil service, the old homeland bureaucracies and the democratic movement. Molefe was surprised because while he had understood that the code was for the civil service, he hadn't realised that people from the parastatals and local and regional governments would also be attending.

The meeting was chaired by a "comrade" from the CSC who explained why there was a need for a code of conduct, and handed out a timetable for the next six months. The first stage of the process was for the members to examine codes from other countries and to consult their constituencies about what should be in the code. Molefe was unsure why they had only been given the codes of conduct of Sweden, the USA and Canada and privately queried how relevant these were to the South African situation. After a few mundane questions the meeting broke up.

Back at the office, Molefe embarked upon his new duties enthusiastically. He was unsure of whom to consult and how, and there was scant precedent. Being from a sound union background, however, he decided that as many people as possible should participate in the process. He therefore organised a series of workshops in the different directorates and, by the next commission meeting, he had a long list of ideas for the code.

At that meeting most of the members had suggestions for the contents of the code, although several had simply regurgitated the examples that they had been given and others had only consulted their superiors. It struck Molefe that the issues raised by the delegates from the local governments and the parastatals were quite different to those suggested by the others. Work progressed and at the end of the six months a comprehensive Code of Conduct had been worked out that incorporated the concerns of most of the Commission members. There were about fifteen items, with some detailed elaboration, and also a few suggestions on how to implement the behavioural maxims.

Molefe felt that, although the process could have been more inclusive, representatives had developed a document that would help to make public servants more effective in their work. He also felt excited about getting back to his permanent job, especially now that he had a better understanding of how other departments and sectors of the civil service operated. He had developed some ideas of how to network with them on manpower issues.

> If you believe that Molefe should hand the Code of Conduct to his superior, Mr Joubert, and return to his previous position, then
> go to POINT THREE.
>
> If you think that he should get involved in implementing the Code within his Department,
> go to POINT FIVE.

POINT 3:

GIVES IT TO SUPERIOR

Molefe felt pleased with himself when he left Mr Joubert's office after giving him the new Code of Conduct. Mr Joubert had been impressed with the document and said that this would definitely make a difference to the ethos of the Department. He also suggested that Molefe might get a promotion or salary increase for his good work. A few days later a copy of the document was sent to every member of the department with a letter from the Director-General asking everyone to read it and apply it as much as possible in their work. The letter also mentioned that a printed version of the Code of Conduct would be coming from the CSC along with further directives concerning ethical conduct. Molefe was surprised at this, as Commission members had not discussed anything other than the Code in the Committee, but he thought the more that was said about ethical conduct, the better.

Although it took a few days to assess what had been happening in his unit in his absence, he soon got back into the full swing of things. When he asked colleagues informally how they had found the Code of Conduct, he got replies such as "I am still wading through it" and "It is a very thorough document but I'm not sure if all of it is relevant to my work".

> Go to questions for discussion

POINT 4:

STAYS IN THE DEPARTMENT

Molefe wasn't sure that he had made the right decision in turning down the assignment, but felt that it really was possible to have some effect in his present job. He continued to strive to instil an ethos of commitment amongst his co-workers, and his unit was soon a shining star in the ministry. However, the unit's role was to work with the different directorates and most of these continued to be inefficient and demotivated. Matters reached a stage where the work of the unit was being frustrated, and the people in it were becoming despondent.

After several meetings on the issue with his superior and the Director-General, Molefe was motivated to try to jolt people out of their apathy. Mr Joubert had suggested he wait until the new Code of Conduct was published but eventually he and the Director-General agreed that Molefe could send a memo around with suggestions of ways in which people could work better. Not surprisingly, this had little effect.

Molefe realised that there was a need for more comprehensive performance-monitoring and evaluation systems. It wasn't the job of his unit to look into these issues but he began to examine ways in which he could use the networks that he was building between the unions, business and the government to monitor the performance of civil servants who dealt directly with the other sectors. He hoped that the good effects of this would ripple through the rest of the ministry. After a number of long, hard-sell meetings with various top officials in the ministry he got the go-ahead to put a plan together.

> Go to questions for discussion

POINT 5:

GETS INVOLVED IN ITS IMPLEMENTATION

When Molefe left Mr Joubert's office he felt that he was on the way up. Mr Joubert was impressed with the document and had agreed to Molefe's request that his unit broaden their role to include developing methods of implementing the code within the ministry. Molefe began by running a series of report-back workshops in the different directorates. He explained the key areas to people and soon realised that the document was too detailed and that not all of it was relevant to a central government department. He then went about developing a summary of the document that he thought would be more useful for the department. After he had run a further series of workshops, it appeared that people had internalised the code and were excited about a new approach to their work. He could see a definite change in attitude through his dealings with people in the normal course of events, and his superior suggested that it was time that he refocused his concentration on his designated duties. After a few months, however, Molefe began to notice people sliding back into old habits and he realised that it was necessary to do something more.

> Go to questions for discussion

QUESTIONS FOR DISCUSSION

1. Why did you make the choices that you did?
2. What are weaknesses of a Code of Conduct?
3. What are the causes of the symptoms that most civil servants in the case exhibited?
4. Are there mechanisms that can be employed against this type of ethos?
5. Is there a conflict between accountability and efficiency and effectiveness in the civil service?

CASE STUDY FOURTEEN

MIKHUKHU PEOPLE OF SOUTH AFRICA: A QUESTION OF SURVIVAL

Rams Ramashia

Mandla Ndlovu is the President of the Mikhukhu People of South Africa (MIPESA), an organisation which was set up in the mid-1980s to look after the interests of people living in informal settlements in South African townships. Over the years, MIPESA has been involved primarily in opposing forced removals of people from these informal settlements as well as fighting landlords who were exploiting residents of backyard shacks. Recently, however, the requests for assistance from these communities had changed: there was an increasing demand for provision of infrastructure and social services in these areas. Members of the executive committee of MIPESA had been trying to convince Mr Ndlovu that outside assistance was needed to enable MIPESA to rise to the challenges it was now facing. Mr Ndlovu remains unconvinced, feeling that the organisation on its own can make the necessary shift in focus.

BACKGROUND

Following the repeal of influx control regulations in the late 1970s, many spouses of migrant labourers and their children left the "homelands" to join their breadwinners in the urban areas. Many other rural men and women, who had hitherto been prohibited from living in the urban areas, flocked to towns and cities around South Africa in search of employment. The flow to the cities had been going on for some years through the consolidation of "homelands" and subsequent evictions of people from so called "black spots" and privately-owned farms, but the repeal of influx control accelerated this migration dramatically.

Cities were unable to cope with the inflow of people into the metropolitan areas as they had not been planned to accommodate such large numbers of black people. The Land Acts and the Group Areas Act had regulated the use of land in favour of whites, and the houses that had been provided in the black townships were insufficient to cope with the large number of people seeking accommodation. During the 1960s, planners had been more concerned with upmarket urban expansion than with provision of housing for the mainly poor black masses who, in any case, had been provided for in the "bantustans".

Those who already had houses in the townships identified this housing crisis as an opportunity to make extra money by filling the vacuum created by State and private sector inactivity. New arrivals were looking for land and they had it. Corrugated iron houses, colloquially known as *mikhukhu* began to spring up in existing residents' backyards. Some landlords had up to five of these dwellings in their backyards. Due to the great demand for these shacks, rentals were very high, ranging from R50 to R100 for nine square meters

Backyards, however, could not accommodate all the families streaming into the townships and *mikhukhu* mushroomed up on every piece of available land, resulting in informal settlements. This phenomenon did not go unnoticed. In 1988, the Minister of Local Government and Housing tabled The Prevention of Squatting Act, which empowered local authorities to forcefully remove and repatriate families who were "illegally squatting" on land not allocated to them by the local authorities. Bulldozers began moving into informal settlements and destroying homes, leaving thousands of families homeless and vulnerable.

It was against this backdrop that people living in informal settlement areas came together to establish MIPESA.

MIPESA

Since its establishment, MIPESA had fought many battles, legal and otherwise. Its constituents had been encouraged to resist removals. It had formed a strong pressure group to demand from local government authorities allocation of land, as well as provision of water and sanitation services for informal settlements. Members of MIPESA had engaged in protest marches to foreign embassies to publicise their plight and to appeal to them for help; and they had actively sought court interdicts against local authorities bulldozing their houses.

MIPESA did not regard provision of social services as its area of focus but soon found itself involved in such projects due to the demands made by its constituency. In one informal settlement area, the organisation provided a clinic through a donation raised from a multinational corporation. In other areas it was instrumental in pressuring authorities into providing schools and educare centres.

While MIPESA was primarily set up to operate in the PWV area, the demand for its services in other areas was very strong and, in a quest to make a national impact, the organisation provided advocacy services to the Botshabelo community in the northern Cape. Another community, which was resettled on a bare piece of land in the eastern Cape, appealed to MIPESA to assist them with raising funds for establishing educare centres, pit-hole toilets and the protection of water springs.

With the repeal of the Prevention of Squatting Act in 1990 the demand for advocacy and protest declined significantly, but many informal communities did not stop demanding MIPESA's attention. Most requests were for the provision of infrastructure and social services. The repeal of the Act finally gave communities some security in the knowledge that they would not be moved from the land they were occupying. Their needs and priorities changed accordingly – from trying to secure tenure to making their areas habitable through ensuring the provision of proper sanitary systems, clean water, educational and health services, and through the creation of jobs.

A SHIFT IN FOCUS

The leadership of MIPESA felt out of its depth as it struggled to deal with new demands. The President, Mr Ndlovu, was a charismatic, rather intimidating man, who was well-liked and respected by his constituency and his executive committee. Although not formally educated, the leader's natural intelligence and understanding of collective behaviour ensured that he received co-operation. The executive committee were somewhat in awe of the leader and seldom disagreed with anything he said or criticised any of his actions. They were willing and eager to carry out his instructions unquestioningly. His strength of character, and defiant attitude had served the organisation well in the days of protest and advocacy, but MIPESA's new role required new skills and strengths. Neither he nor any of the members of the executive committee had had any experience in running a service organisation.

MIPESA had, over the years, established solid contacts in the private sector and with foreign embassies. These contacts seemed willing to fund MIPESA in its new role as provider of social services, but made it clear that MIPESA would need to reorganise its administration and redefine its mission statement.

MIPESA had to work quickly. Two other organisations had sprung up in informal settlements: one aligned to the IFP and the other to the ANC, and both were pressuring MIPESA members to shift their allegiance away from the leader. Their efforts had been largely unsuccessful, and most remained loyal, but now rumours about MIPESA had begun to emanate from MIPESA members of civic associations aligned to the "Mass Democratic Movement" to the effect that MIPESA was mismanaging and embezzling funds raised in the name of the poor. The people were beginning to ask questions.

MIPESA had by this time managed to set up a small office in Braamfontein with the help of a grant from the Swiss Embassy. The grant had been small and was sufficient to cover only the rental and to purchase a desk and a typewriter. The President of MIPESA served as the National Co-ordinator on a voluntary basis and two other volunteers served as field workers. Further funding was urgently needed to employ people on a full-time basis. Many of the projects which MIPESA had set up, such as brick-making and sewing projects, as well as the poultry-farming and shoe-repair co-ops were on the point of collapse due to lack of resources and poor management.

Realising that MIPESA is faced with the possibility of becoming ineffective and even extinct, Mr Ndlovu reluctantly admits that the problems and challenges facing the organisation at this stage are too complex for him to solve single-handedly. He decides to heed the advice of the members of his executive committee and to call on outside assistance.

Mr Ndlovu empowers his Management Committee to look around for a suitable NGO Management Consultant to help MIPESA, and they call in your consultancy to advise them on what steps are needed to deal with their problems.

EXERCISE

How would you go about helping MIPESA to solve its problem?
1. Draw up a document outlining the strategy you have devised to ensure MIPESA's survival including the new administrative structure and mission statement.
2. Draw up a funding document for submission to ensure MIPESA's survival including the new administrative structure and mission statement.
3. Draw up a funding document for submission to prospective donors to ensure MIPESA's financial sustainability.

CASE STUDY FIFTEEN

WATER, WATER EVERYWHERE AND NOT A DROP TO DRINK

Andries van Rooyen

1

Dennis Roberts, the Town Engineer of Bracken East, sat hunched on his bed with his head in his hands. It was 06h08 on Sunday 27 December 1993, the dawn of a pleasant summer morning. The telephone call Dennis had just received from one of his standby staff, telling him that the Twin Peaks residential area was without water supply, confirmed his worst fears. He was thinking back to the numerous reports he had submitted to Council about the defects in the water system and his recommendations that Council give priority to this as a matter of urgency. Dennis jumped when his phone rang again at 06h10.

Dennis: "This is 55 8866, Dennis Roberts speaking."
Voice: "Dennis, this is Chris Masson." (Chris Masson is the Mayor of Bracken East and also a councillor for Ward Two, of which Twin Peaks forms a part.)
Dennis: "Morning, Sir, how are you and how can I be of assistance?"
Chris: "Dennis, listen, there is apparently no water supply in the suburb of Twin Peaks and you chaps will have to do something about the matter immediately. I am being pestered by telephone calls from the early risers in the area who are really hot under the collar because of this breakdown of service. I need answers..."
Dennis: "Sorry to interrupt, Sir, but you know very well that I have on numerous occasions reported to Council..."
Chris: "Listen, Dennis, this is not the time to ponder on what should have been done. You people are the experts and I expect immediate action. We owe it to the ratepayers. Please phone me within half an hour to tell me what your plan of action is going to be. Goodbye."
Dennis: "Yes, Sir. Goodbye, Sir".

Dennis was frustrated and worried. The Mayor was well aware of the concerns he as Town Engineer had expressed in a number of technical reports to Council pertaining to the town's water supply system. His staff were also well informed on the necessary precautionary measures to follow in monitoring the water service delivery. What had gone wrong?

2

The fast-developing and bustling town of Bracken East is situated in an area well-known for its pleasant climate and abundance of water resources. These features, coupled with the record of the Bracken East Town Council for providing services of an excellent standard, have played a role in stimulating the growth of the town. Evidence of this growth is the doubling of its residents over the past five years.

Bracken East is also known for the breathtaking panoramic views which can be enjoyed from the suburbs on the mountainsides rising steeply from the relative flatness of the town centre. While the topography affords dramatic views, it also makes great demands on the supply of water by the Bracken East Town Council. All water, other than that supplied to the lower-lying area in the vicinity of the business centre, must be pumped to higher levels. In such a system there are several restraints, namely:

- The limitation to the height to which pumps can lift water requires that it be lifted in stages. At each stage a reservoir has to be built to ensure a supply of water for pumping up to the next stage.
- A reservoir is used to supply water to an area in its vicinity called a zone; this zone must be carefully selected, particularly under circumstances of very steep gradients. The pressure at the properties concerned must not be too low at the upper boundary of the zone and it must not be too high at the lower boundary of the zone. It is desirable that a reservoir should have a capacity to store a 48-hour supply for the area it is to serve.
- A pumping system is very vulnerable in that:
  - pumps, being mechanical tools, can, even with the best of maintenance programmes, break down without notice; it is therefore desirable that every pump station should house at least one standby pump;
  - the electric motors driving the pump can burn out, especially if they have to run continuously for long periods on end and it is therefore desirable that a replacement motor should be available;
  - the electricity supply can be interrupted; and
  - there can be a fault in the pipe used to pump water to a higher level known as the "rising main".

The Bracken East water supply system has four subsystems, at three of which the water requires to be pumped upwards. The conditions prevailing at the three are typical of a system which grew by ad hoc extensions to meet immediate demands rather than from any attempt at co-ordinated planning. The critical elements in this respect are:

- the pump capacities are inadequate, with the result that pumps sometimes run continually for as long as 18 hours out of 24; pumps and motors cannot take such strain and a total collapse during a dry spell with disastrous consequences, is not unlikely; there is, furthermore, no standby facility;
- some of the rising mains are inadequate;

- although rising main bursts and electrical faults cannot be avoided, a system should be flexible enough so that any area can be supplied from the reservoir of another area until repairs have been carried out – this is generally not the case in Bracken East.
- the design of one of the pump stations, namely that at Twin Peaks, is of such a nature that the pipe supplying the reticulated area is also used to supply water to the pump; and
- there is no monitoring system of reservoir levels and total reliance is on physical inspection.

3

When Dennis Roberts joined the service of the Bracken East Town Council three years ago as Town Engineer, he immediately put his practical expertise to work in fully acquainting himself with the state of the service delivery of the department for which he was responsible. It did not take him long, with the help of his staff, to realise that the existing water supply system had a number of latent systemic defects which, if not monitored closely, could lead to a breakdown in service delivery to some areas of the town. Within three months of his appointment he had submitted a comprehensive report to Council in which he outlined these systemic defects, highlighting the grave possibility of a breakdown in service. The report proposed that Council appoint a firm of consultants to conduct a comprehensive study of the town's water supply system and to report on an integrated plan for the system which would eliminate the critical elements on each supply line and ensure the flexibility to deal with emergencies in any particular area. The critical elements to be investigated were:
- adequate pump and motor capacity, and standbys;
- adequate rising main capacities;
- upgrading of the electrical supply to pump-stations and the suitability of the switch-gear;
- adequate reservoir capacities;
- improvements to the pump-station design; and
- the estimated cost to implement the recommendations.

4

The consultants identified as top priority the upgrading of rising main capacities and the provision of larger pumps and pipes in certain areas. The expenditure to effect this improvement was estimated at R1,3 million. In support of the consultant's report, the Town Engineer recommended that Council resolve to allocate the required funds in the next budget, which was being prepared at the time, and that the work commence as a matter of urgency. Council, however, decided

not to accept the recommendations of the Town Engineer, and to postpone a decision on the matter for a year. Reflecting on the discussion during the Council meeting, Dennis Roberts concluded that Council was influenced in its decision by:
- the fact that a breakdown in the water supply had hitherto not occurred;
- the strong stance of the Mayor in favour of the allocation of funds (which was approved) for the upgrading of parks – a service improvement for which local inhabitants had been clamouring for quite some time; and
- the imminence of the municipal elections scheduled to take place within two months.

5

Dennis Roberts was confronted with a problem on two levels. Most immediately, the Twin Peaks residential area was, at this moment, without water and something would have to be done urgently. But getting the town's abundant water supply to the higher lying residential areas was an ongoing concern. Dennis was confident that he could do something about the immediate problem but the time had surely come to think of a manageable, long-term solution. Perhaps he should get the council to view the whole question as a policy issue, rather than just an engineering "hassle". He wondered whether he, pigeon-holed as a "technical expert", would be able to do that.

PUTTING RESPONSIBILITY WHERE IT FITS: A QUESTION OF MOTIVATION AT TIVUMBA HOSPITAL

Lauren Blythe Schütte

INTRODUCTION

In late September, Hans Kuiter, Medical Officer in Charge (MO i/c) at Tivumba Hospital began to draw up the agenda for October's Management Committee meeting. In addition to the standard items which appeared every month, there were two important issues which had to be discussed at this meeting. The first was the future of the hospital's primary health care programme and the second was the compilation of the Annual Report.

Both these matters had been giving Kuiter many anxious moments. The first was bound to cause conflict as no one seemed able to agree on the hospital's priorities, and it would clearly be an ongoing debate. The Annual Report was another problem which never seemed to go away: it was always completed months after the deadline and Hans was determined not to see a repeat of this situation. This year the Annual Report had taken on greater significance, as one of the hospital's main donors was demanding to know how their money had been utilised before renewing any pledges of assistance. What Hans really wanted to achieve at the forthcoming meeting was a commitment from all heads of department to take responsibility for accurate and timeous completion of the Annual Report.

ADDED RESPONSIBILITY

Hans was a Dutch expatriate who had spent three frustrating years working at Tivumba Hospital. As the months wore on he had found himself taking on an ever-increasing workload in the face of what he considered to be a general lack of motivation amongst hospital personnel. He regularly went home tired and dejected. His wife, Inger, would often hear stories of Hans' disappointments when things had not worked out as he would have liked them to and she had tried to get through to him that he was not the only person responsible for keeping the hospital running smoothly. But Hans had always found delegation difficult and had had to learn to live with the consequences.

A year ago, Hans had been promoted to MO i/c, when this position was vacated by another Dutch expatriate, Jan Rabie. Hans' new position involves him in all three decision making bodies at the hospital: the Board of Governors; the Management Committee and the Daily Board. **The Daily Board** consisting of himself, the Nursing Officer in charge and the Administrator, is responsible for the daily running of the hospital. The **Management Committee** meets on a monthly basis and is concerned with the general management of the hospital. It consists of the following members:

- *The Management Committee:*
  Medical Officer i/c
  Nursing Officer i/c
  Tutor i/c
  Administrator
  Head Technical Department
  Trade Union Representative (currently the head of the laboratory)

Hans is also involved in the highest authority in the hospital – the **Board of Governors** – which discusses issues beyond the competence and authority of the Management Committee, such as approval of the budget which has to be submitted to the government. Members of the governing board have been expressing their concern over the tardiness of the submission of the Annual Report and doubts have been cast on Hans' ability to get things done.

Hans is sensitive about these criticisms. Despite his involvement in all three decision-making bodies at the hospital he has found acting as MO i/c very difficult. He is often surprised by the ways in which decisions affect various workers at the hospital. There are many personal interests at stake and hidden nuances to take into consideration and, as an expatriate, Hans often feels that he lacks the necessary background to make sound decisions.

MOTIVATING THE MANAGEMENT COMMITTEE

Hans hoped to alert members of the Management Committee to the importance of the Annual Report at the forthcoming meeting. He was concerned not only with the tardy completion of the report in previous years but also its accuracy. Delays had been caused by completely unreliable in-patient and out-patient figures and, as for the laboratory figures, they were three to four times higher than they should have been! Heads of departments were, of course, officially responsible for the compilation of departmental statistics and progress reports, whilst the MO i/c was responsible only for compiling the final product. However, for various reasons, the MO i/c had traditionally come to bear the responsibility for the entire report. Last year, in the absence of any co-operation from heads of departments, Hans had found himself burdened with the time-consuming task of recounting, recalculating and reclassifying all the figures that had been submitted, and gathering those that hadn't. He had spent many nights burning the midnight oil in an attempt to verify the figures and to bash the report into a reasonable format. He felt that this task had impacted on his ability to perform his other responsibilities effectively and had given him a bad reputation with the Board of Governors.

As always, lack of motivation was the problem, he thought to himself. He had no intention of letting the same thing happen this year. The members of the Management Committee would have to share the burden. He leaned back in his chair and thought about his colleagues on the committee and wondered whose support he could count on for the task at hand. There were many personalities involved and meetings were often fraught with clashes of interest which impacted on the Committee's ability to function as an effective decision-making body. He anticipated the usual disagreements over hospital priorities and the allocation of resources. He pondered over how he could structure the agenda in order to minimise conflict over broader issues and get commitment on the immediate objective: the timeous completion of the Annual Report. He thought first of his colleagues who shared the responsibility for the daily running of the hospital: Mavis and Simon.

Mavis

Mavis Ndebele was the Nursing Officer in Charge (NO i/c). She had a long history with the hospital, having worked there for the past 20 years. Hans worked closely with her in the daily running of the hospital and had noticed that, although she was not always the first to speak up when decisions needed to be taken, her contributions were listened to carefully and appreciated by everyone. Hans had been impressed by her performance and valued her assistance. Although they were both in agreement on the hospital's priorities (that intramural care had to be prioritised and that other programmes such as primary health care, whilst valuable and necessary, should be regarded as additional), Hans had learned that her attitude to the Dutch doctors was not always positive and this worried him. Every two years, a new Dutch doctor took over as MO i/c and she was obviously tired of having to listen to their new ideas and new proposals. She made it clear that she thought that, because they were not going to stay on, they should stick to medical work and not interfere with internal management. He was not sure of her co-operation and wondered how he could get it.

Simon

Hans' thoughts moved on to the Administrator, Simon Madinane. For five years, Simon had been a reliable and efficient Administrator and had kept spending well within budgets. His success on this front had, however, brought him into conflict with other members of the Management Committee, for instance the Head of the Technical Department who seemed incapable of working within its allocated budget. Simon worried about the constant stream of accounts for repairs to equipment and cars and told Hans that he thought there was little excuse for hiring external skilled workers to do jobs which should have been done by the department. He had made it clear that he believed that the way the department was organised had a lot to do with its failure to keep within budget. There were bound to be some clashes and Hans knew that he would have to manage this conflict in order to achieve his objective. Hans also knew that Simon was committed to extending the hospital's primary health care programme and was concerned about the lack of clear policy on this issue and how this impacted on hospital budgets. Simon was bound to push for some resolution on this issue and Hans wondered how he could get him to focus on the more immediate one: the Annual Report.

SETTING THE AGENDA

Hans needed to convince the committee of the importance of producing an excellent Annual Report but he knew that the order of agenda items would influence the outcome of the meeting and thus his ability to succeed. If he listed the hospital's primary health programme before the Annual Report he might risk alienating Simon in his support for Mavis on this issue. On the other hand, if he didn't first tackle the issues that were worrying committee members, they might not pay as much attention to the Annual Report issue as Hans wanted them to. He wondered what his strategy for the meeting should be and how he should arrange the agenda items in order to minimise conflict over broader issues in order to gain co-operation on the Annual Report.

CASE STUDY SEVENTEEN

BELLROW MUNICIPALITY HOUSING DEPARTMENT: AN IN-BASKET EXERCISE

Erwin Schwella

GENERAL BACKGROUND

Bellrow is a South African local authority in a large metropolitan complex. The inhabitants of the area total approximately 105 000. According to latest official census figures there are approximately 40 000 brown, 30 000 white and 35 000 black citizens. The white citizens are housed in formal housing generally owned by them. The majority of brown citizens live in their own houses but about 30% still rent houses presently administered by Council. About 90% of the black citizens are newly urbanised and have erected their own structures on a piece of land adjoining the historically brown area. This land came under Bellrow's jurisdiction following the local government restructuring of 1994.

Bellrow City Council has 24 members. Of these, 14 were elected on the basis of wards, half of which represent the black community and half the other communities. The remaining 10 members were elected on a basis of proportional representation by the community as a whole. The present political and interest group support is as follows:

- Newsa African Liberation Congress (NALC):   8
- Newsa National party (NNP):   6
- Africanist Movement Party (AMP):   2
- Newsa Independent Civic Organisation (NICO):   1
- Federation of Ratepayers Associations (FRA):   4
- Independents: 3

Shifting issue alliances have made the decision-making fluid and there is a fair balance of power in Council.

Bellrow has developed rapidly in the past decade due, *inter alia*, to its close proximity to the city core and to large industrial areas developed by Bellrow Municipality and private industrialists.

Bellrow's rapid development, as well as the incorporation of the black townships into Bellrow, has increased the demand for residential plots as well as for housing schemes that can provide rented accommodation for the large number of workers in the industrial areas.

Bellrow Municipality accepted this challenge and developed, in liaison with the relevant central governmental departments, a number of housing schemes to meet with the most pressing needs of the various communities. There are however still serious shortages, especially in sub-economic housing for the less wealthy inhabitants.

At present the Municipality administers one large cluster-housing complex consisting of 3 000 units which are inhabited by those who can afford low to average payments. Rental is calculated on a scale according to the income of the tenant. The Municipality also administers various sub-economic housing schemes amounting to 10 000 units. At present 4 000 more such units are being built in one of the areas. These units were planned carefully with the aid of a multidisciplinary team to incorporate functionality with economy without giving the impression of uniformity. Indications are that the new scheme will be very popular but perhaps a bit too expensive for the intended market.

PERSONNEL PARTICULARS

André Johnson: Director of Housing Bellrow Municipality

You, André Johnson, are the present incumbent in this position in the Department of the Town Clerk. You report directly on all housing matters to the Deputy Town Clerk who is the head of the department. Although you are bound by all statutory provisions regarding local government administration in general, and housing matters in particular, the style of the Deputy Town Clerk and the attitude of the Council is to allow you to handle most issues that arise with regard to the Housing Branch on your own.

You have been in this position for about two years. Prior to this you had fifteen years of experience in various other positions within local authorities. During this period you completed a Bachelor's degree through correspondence, majoring in Economics and Sociology. You are presently enrolled for an MPA at a local university. You are now 36 years old.

Information is provided about your secretary, the housing officer, who your deputy is, and the assistant housing officer. The rest of your staff consists of 30 people, including clerical and maintenance staff and collectors.

Ms Minnie Brown: Secretary to the Director of Housing

Ms Minnie Brown has been working in the Housing Branch as Secretary for ten years and is very valuable because of her experience regarding housing matters. She is a widow of fifty-three, with a wit as sharp as her secretarial skills. You have always felt very comfortable in dealing with her.

Hank Skinner: Housing Officer

Hank Skinner is forty-eight, married and has two children. His wife is related to a former Member of Parliament for the Bellrow constituency who still has influence in political circles. Hank – who is your deputy – has been the Housing Officer for ten years. He holds no post-matric qualification. He applied for the position of

Director of Housing but you were appointed. He is reasonably effective in his job but hints at using his "contacts" when the going gets tough.

Bill Mnisi: Assistant Housing Officer

Bill Mnisi has an I.A.C.-diploma and is working towards a degree in social work. He was appointed to the position of Assistant Housing Officer as part of an affirmative action programme instituted by the Council three years ago. He has been with the Branch for two years after a stint of five years with an NGO involved with community development. He has potential as a worker but his real interest is working for his church. He seems frustrated by the fact that his work does not involve him more closely with people. His primary function is the allocation of housing units to new applicants. Generally he has been trustworthy and consistent.

ANDRÉ JOHNSON'S IN-BASKET

Today is Saturday. You, André, have just returned from a SA Institute of Housing conference on community development in Port Elizabeth which lasted two days and, while stopping at the office for your mail, you decide to clean up your in-basket in preparation for what you know will be an exhausting week.

Respond to each of the items you find in your basket in an appropriate way.

IN-BASKET ITEM NO 1

MEMO

FROM: Ms Minnie Brown, Secretary
TO: ANDRÉ JOHNSON (HOUSING DIRECTOR)

Mr Johnson

Councillor Piet Willemse, the chairman of the Housing Committee, came by here yesterday with the following cutting from the local newspaper. He has received a number of phone calls about the matter since the publication on the day before yesterday and is more than a little disturbed by it. He requested that you take appropriate action to rectify matters.

I would also like to draw to your attention that Councillor Willemse's term of office expires in October and that he plans to stand for re-election in November.

MINNIE

IN-BASKET ITEM NO 1(A)

BELLROW TIMES

WITHOUT HOUSE, BELLROW, writes: Together with thousands I want to complain about the housing needs of coloureds within the Bellrow area. Many want to acquire their own homes but are not able to do so. For this reason they have to suffer under high rentals every month.

Despite the needs of our group that are being overlooked it is being reported that 4 000 more houses are being erected in the previously black townships for rental to other groups at very low rates. Why is it that our group always has to get the worst deal in this town while thousands of houses are being erected with the use of tax-payers' money for rental to other groups?

I would like to remind the Bellrow City Council that our group makes a great contribution to taxes, but that expenditure is not appropriated accordingly. Some of the other groups contribute very little to the municipal chest, but they get benefits. I want to call on citizens to remember that Council elections will be held during November and that something will have to be done about the situation.

IN-BASKET ITEM NO 2

THE XY CHURCH OF S.A. (EAST BELLROW PARISH)

TELEPHONE: 21572
P.O. BOX 276
BELLROW, 6666

The Housing Director
Bellrow Municipality
P.O. Box 1
Bellrow, 6666

Sir

ALLOCATION OF HOUSES

I have been instructed by the Council of my church to write to you about the allocation of houses in our parish by the Municipality.

It has been established that out of ten houses allocated to applicants during the previous two months, five were allocated to members of the AB church, three to people who do not even belong to a church and only two to members of XY church. It has also been noticed that one of your employees, Mr Bill Mnisi, is involved with activities of AB church. The Council feels that this "coincidence" warrants investigation.

In the meantime it is felt that the next allocations should go to members of our church to compensate for seeming discrimination in the past.

Your kind consideration and speedy reply is appreciated.

Yours faithfully
S. PETERSEN (SCRIBE)

IN-BASKET ITEM NO 3

MEMO

FROM: ERNST SEEGERS (DEPUTY TOWN CLERK)
TO: ANDRÉ JOHNSON (HOUSING DIRECTOR)

INVITATION TO ADDRESS MEETING OF MIELIEBLAAR CLUB

André

The Mielieblaar Club has extended an invitation for any suitable speaker to address the club on the housing policy of Council at the Lekkerbly Hotel on 27th of this month.
I would appreciate your motivated ideas on:

a) whether we should accept,
b) who should attend, and
c) what you think we should convey if we do attend.

I would like to mention that the Mielieblaar Club is known to have sympathy with rightist political groups. Bear in mind that Councillors Pieters, Rudolph and Viljoen have links with the Mielieblaar Club.

Signed
E. Seegers

IN-BASKET ITEM NO 4

5 Piet Retief Road
Bellrow
2 April

The Housing Director
Bellrow Municipality
P.O. Box 1
Bellrow

Dear Mr Johnson

I noticed that you advertise a position for a housing assistant in your Department. I was advised by my niece who is married to Hank Skinner, the Housing Officer in your Department, to write to you before applying.

If I do get this job it will be like a new beginning for me. I am willing to accept this rather humble position although I hold a B.Bus.Sc. degree.

You see while at university I started using very mild quantities of a habit-forming medicinal drug. After having finished my degree at Southern University I worked for four companies and gained valuable experience. At present I am unemployed after having been to a rehabilitation centre for the use of drugs. I have been fully rehabilitated and can also state that I have since become a member of the faith. This will be confirmed by Dr. Swart, my psychiatrist, and Mr. Jansen, our religious leader.

I am thus interested in using my talents to the benefit of your organisation, but would like to hear what the Council's views are on appointing people like myself before applying formally.

Finally I have to state that I am 27 years old, grew up in Bellrow and still consider myself a loyal citizen.

I hope to hear from you soon.

R. KNOETZE

IN-BASKET ITEM NO 5

S.T. BUCK CARTAGE.

605 Ravens Road
Industrial Park
Bellrow
6666

Mr André Johnson
Housing Director
Bellrow Municipality
P.O. Box 1
Bellrow
6666

Dear Mr Johnson

As you will probably recall we have several times tendered for municipal contracts for delivering goods and the selling of sand and quarry stone for use in the housing schemes of this city. We used to have a very good relationship with your Housing Officer Mr Hank Skinner when he acted in your present position after the sudden death of your predecessor. We would like to establish as cordial a relationship with you. We therefore would like you to attend a dinner with us whenever it suits you.

We hope to be able to discuss business at such an opportunity. Kindly let us know what date will suit you.

In the past we have loyally supported the sitting members of Council for this ward through the local ratepayers association.

Hoping to hear from you soon.

Sincerely yours
ABE STRAUSS (OWNER)

IN-BASKET ITEM NO 6

FACSIMILE TRANSMISSION

FROM: NALC BRANCH BELLROW
TO: HOUSING OFFICER, BELLROW MUNICIPALITY

This is to inform you that our local branch considered the new housing project being erected in our area at present at our most recent meeting. We have registered our strongest possible concern with our party representatives on Council about the following matters:

- the size of the houses being erected seems to be too small for families of 6 people and more,
- the possibility that some of the houses could be allocated to people presently residing in other areas of Bellrow and who have not suffered as much as we have,
- the process of allocation of these houses which we believe should be done in consultation with us as being the majority party represented in Council.

We have requested Councillor Ndabazandile, our party leader in Council, to collect your opinions on these questions for us in writing. He will contact you during next week to arrange picking up the document from you.

Signed: P. MDUZA
Chairperson

CASE STUDY EIGHTEEN

10111 –
THE SOWETO FLYING SQUAD

Jacqui Myburgh

"There can be no New South Africa without us!" exclaimed Colonel J. H. Deyzel, Commanding Officer of the Soweto Flying Squad. The case-writer had just asked what the future would hold for 10111 in the "New South Africa".

"We are here to stay," he said, indicating the operations office with a wave of his hand. The room was roughly 6 x 4 meters. It contained a few large desks and grey chairs, as well as some electronic gadgets. In the corner were four large filing cabinets, boldly labelled ALPHA, BRAVO, CHARLIE and DELTA. Above the door was a huge red STOP sign, a gift from the traffic department. Behind the door was a smaller room with sound-proof walls. The case-writer's eyes fell on a collection of porcelain and plastic turtles in various shades of green on the top of the filing cabinet. The Colonel remarked proudly, "Oh! That's my collection."

The Colonel took the case-writer to the smaller control room. The silence in the room was broken from time to time by the telephone ringing, followed later by scratchy voices as officers barked instructions into their high-frequency radios.

"This is the 'nerve centre' of the Soweto Flying Squad," stated the Colonel, proudly. The case-writer thought back to the early 1970s days before television was introduced, when Friday Night's "Squad Cars" was one of the most popular radio programmes. He recalled the introduction to the programme, and chuckled to himself: "They prowl the empty streets at night, waiting, in fast cars, on foot, living with crime and violence. These are the men of South Africa. These are the men of SQUAD CARS".

BACKGROUND

10111 is the emergency telephone number for the South African Police (SAP) Flying Squad service. It is a geographically zoned dial-free number. In other words, if a caller dials the number, it is relayed to the nearest control centre, and it costs the caller nothing. The system has been in operation, country wide since the late 1970s.

Colonel Deyzel joined the police force in 1965 and served in various police stations before taking command of the Flying Squad in Soweto, colloquially known as, 10111. The case-writer asked him why the number 10111 was selected, and not a number such as 911 or 999. The Colonel stood up, disappeared into the next office and came back with a disconnected dial-type telephone. He then demonstrated how easy it was for a frightened person to remember and dial the number. Since 1 and 0 were at the extremes of the dial, the number could be dialled even in darkness.

The Soweto Flying Squad unit was set up in Protea Police Station in January 1990, with the following main objective:

> "To supply an efficient and effective policing unit for Soweto, Lenasia and Eldorado Park communities. This is achieved by immediate attention to complaints and a fast reaction time".

(See Appendix 1 for the organisation chart.)

SOWETO

The name Soweto is an acronym for the South Western Townships of Johannesburg, a sprawling mass of houses about 15 km South-West of Johannesburg. The name was adopted in 1963. In January of that year, *The Star* newspaper reported that:

> "an effort to give the African Townships of Johannesburg an identity of their own and rid them of the impersonal name of South Western Bantu Townships is being made by the City Council. A special committee has waded through hundreds of suggestions and recommended five – Soweto, Sawesko, Swestown, Phaphama Villages and Partheid Townships. The Council's Non-European Affairs Department considers one of the first two names suitable. Other suggestions that did not find favour included Verwoerdstad and Hendrik Verwoerdville".

Soweto is too big to be considered a town, but it does not have the urban amenities of a city. This is a consequence of apartheid legislation, particularly in the 1950s when the government actively discouraged the establishment of amenities such as old age homes, orphanages, clinics and shops.

The history of Soweto is linked to the history of Johannesburg. Johannesburg started off as a mining camp in the late 1800s and within 10 years the population had grown to over 80 000 people, half of whom were black. Many blacks and whites lived together in a squalid area on the western side of town. The Western Native Township was established in 1918 on the site, and the township grew from then on. When bubonic plague broke out in 1940, the black inhabitants were resettled in an emergency camp at Klipspruit, near the future Soweto. When the Nationalist Party came into power, there was a concerted effort to segregate Soweto into zones for each of the different ethnic groups, and to adhere to a policy that Soweto would serve only as temporary accommodation for the black working class.

Soweto is ethnically diversified, but because of the past official policy regarding allocation of housing and restriction in mobility and choice, the spatial distribution of its people has tended to follow ethnic rather than economic lines. Therefore, there are middle and upper-middle class families living together with lower-class and very poor families.

The township has had a long history of politically motivated violence and unrest, mainly due to people's resistance to oppressive apartheid policies. In addition, the township is also reputed to have one of the highest crime rates in the world. One of the worst periods was during the uprisings in 1976, when school children protested against the use of Afrikaans as a medium of instruction. The uprising was ruthlessly suppressed by the police and the military, and made world headlines. It was widely publicised that the police had opened fire on a 6 000-strong crowd of schoolchildren. Thereafter, the presence of the military and police in the townships became a way of life.

The 1980s were characterised by rent boycotts, which had a crippling financial effect on town councils. The initial response of the council was to evict people whose rent was in arrears. The evictions were carried out by the police and the military. The response from the community was to remove street names and house numbers so that they could not be easily traced. The evictions were later stopped by a Supreme Court ruling. In addition, there were a number of uprisings in the schools in the 1980s, and 1985 emerged as another year of violent action in the townships. The people's court emerged, and so-called "sell-outs" to the government and police were publicly tried and executed by "necklacing" (a tyre is placed around the neck of the accused, doused with petrol and set alight). The police were criticised during this time for their lack of intervention. There were often reports that they stood by passively while "necklacings" took place.

In 1989, a new type of violence erupted in Soweto when hundreds of people lost their lives because of faction fighting between two main groups, Xhosas and Zulus. Major political organisations such as the African National Congress (ANC), the Inkatha Freedom Party (IFP) and the Pan Africanist Congress (PAC), were implicated in the fighting, with claims that the battle was mainly between the allies of the ANC and Inkatha. Police were accused of taking the side of Inkatha in the fighting. These claims further strained the relations between the police and the residents.

In 1994, the first democratic elections were held in South Africa and whilst political violence decreased somewhat, criminal violence continued unabated.

HOW 10111 OPERATES IN SOWETO

When a call comes in, it is answered by one of the staff in the operations room. The caller is first asked to describe the nature of the emergency, and then for the address or the area of the crime or problem. He or she may remain anonymous if desired. The details are recorded by hand on a standard form by the telephone operator. The operator assigns a serial number to the form and an emergency classification code, and then passes it to the supervisor on the radio control unit. Depending on the classification of the emergency, the radio control operator may call up the patrol cars and send the car closest to the area to investigate.

The Soweto operations room is equipped with eight separate telephone units, chairs and desks. There is a frequency radio control unit, a computer (which is used to record vehicle thefts) and a big wall map of the area, facing both operators. During off-peak times, there are just two telephones, two radios, two operators and a supervisor in the control room. Six patrol cars operate in the field.

States Colonel Deyzel:

> "Say, for example, car Tango India 21 responds. The radio operator will explain to the patrol the nature of the complaint, where the incident has taken place, and issue if suspects are armed. The Flying Squad will move into the area, either with blaring sirens or silently (depending on the nature of the emergency), and attend to the complaint. Sometimes they arrest a culprit, and then radio back a report to the Flying Squad Headquarters in Soweto."

Sometimes the 10111 cars are stopped in the streets and asked to respond to an emergency on the spot.

DEMAND ON THE SYSTEM

Shortly after the service was introduced, it handled 90 complaints per week. This has increased to an average of 65 calls per day under normal circumstances (i.e. when there is no unrest) and 150 calls per day during peak periods. The average time between a call being received to a patrol arriving at the scene (the reaction time) is 23 minutes. According to Colonel Deyzel, this does not compare well with the first-world standard of 2 minutes' reaction time. It takes no more than 30 seconds for a telephone to be answered and no more than 15 seconds to contact a patrol vehicle.

The Colonel feels that six cars are just a drop in the ocean and would dearly like the unit to have more cars. He is of the opinion that the unit could be more effective with four times its present staff.

During winter months there is generally a decline in the average number of calls per day. The colonel continued,

> "Weather is the best policeman. For example, on cold or rainy days we receive very few calls. Hot summer nights are a problem. Monday is quiet. Wednesday night is very busy; we call it 'Klein Saterdag' (small Saturday). Friday night is called 'Boxing Day' because most of the calls on Friday night are about street fights. From 13h00 on Saturdays until about 21h00 hours on Sunday, we are at our peak. I think it is because people drink throughout the night."

MANAGEMENT OF CAPACITY

The incoming calls are rated. For example, if a caller says that there are strange people in his/her yard, or that someone is breaking into his/her house, this gets a priority rating. "Boxing match calls" get the lowest rating. We respond to them immediately only when there are free patrol cars available. Patrols are often redirected from low to high priority calls.

The staff in the Soweto operations' room are able to operate all the equipment – radio control staff can attend to incoming calls.

During Saturdays, an additional telephone operator is employed. Although the unit has only six cars, it has access to other cars at the station. Cars at other police stations often help during emergencies.

Callers during peak time will be answered, but are often asked to hold for some time before an operator is free to take down details of the complaint.

SOWETO FLYING SQUAD STAFF

The Soweto staff is multiracial. The working environment is informal and people address each other on first name terms. According to the Colonel, they regard themselves as friends more than as work colleagues. To stress the point the Colonel recalled,

> "In September 1990, one of our cars, responding to a false emergency, was ambushed in Diepkloof. My men were fired at with AK-47s. One of them, a white officer, died. At his funeral the black guys were crying more than the white guys, because they didn't just lose a colleague, they also lost a friend. There is no racial friction. They do the wrong things together and I punish them together. Sometimes, you've got to be reactive, discipline them the hard way in order to motivate them."

In addition to the normal police training, there is an on-going in-house training programme. Sometimes the staff members are sent on external courses.

Meetings are held regularly, giving staff members a chance to share their experiences and exchange ideas with their colleagues and seniors.

> "Effective allocation of staff is a problem," Colonel Deyzel continued. "You see, there are two types of policeman. There is a policeman who would not like to spend his time answering telephones or working with computers, the type who prefers to be in the field where there is action. Behind the computer he is useless. You also have the opposite type."

WHAT THE STAFF SAID

During a coffee break, the case-writer decided to interview two operating Soweto Flying Squad staff members:

Q: What are the objectives of 10111?

A: *To respond to complaints and emergencies as quickly as possible and to deliver a professional service to the people of Soweto.*

Q: What are your particular roles?

A: *To serve and protect at all times, by being in charge of the Flying Squad shift.*

Q: What problems do you encounter in providing the service?

A: House numbers and street names were removed during the 1976 riots and the rent boycott in the late eighties. Sometimes just looking for a house number takes close to an hour.

The zones are also not marked and numbers are duplicated. For example there is house number 200 in each zone in Meadowlands. If you cross the street, you may be crossing from one zone to another without being aware of it.

The roads are bad and, as a result, the patrol cars frequently get punctures.

We often get false complaints, mainly from children.

At times the community interferes with our work by preventing the arrest of a suspect.

Q: How do you think you are perceived by the community?

A: In general, I think we are well perceived.

Q: How do you think the community evaluates the 10111 service?

A: It depends. For example, if your car is stolen and we recover it, then you will say 10111 is great. But if your brother drives a stolen car and refuses to stop, and I shoot him, you are not going to like the Flying Squad.

Q: How does the unit compare with other units?

A: I cannot say we are a better unit than others, I can only say we are a special unit. If you join this unit you must be a full-blooded policeman, have the right character and be willing to work very hard in risky situations for long hours.

Q: What are relations like between staff members?

A: In this unit we work more or less as a family. I think it is because we live in danger all the time. We depend on each other, that is why we are so close.

INFORMING THE COMMUNITY ABOUT 10111 IN SOWETO

"I believe that police visibility is an effective anti-crime weapon," continued the Colonel. "When I took command of the unit in January 1990, all Flying Squad cars were unmarked regular yellow police cars. I recommended that all the unit cars, be clearly marked and identifiable as 10111 Emergency Police Flying Squad. This was done and it helped to create public awareness of the service. Other units throughout the country soon followed."

He feels that public response has been positive.

"When a 10111 car passes in Soweto, it is common to hear teenagers shouting 'Viva Golf GTI! Viva 10111! Viva Flying Squad!' People who have been helped also spread the word about the availability of the service. We, as a unit, don't advertise in the media. However, the police force is trying to improve its image, and there was an advert on TV1, 2, 3 and 4 showing police playing soccer with a multi-racial group of children."

When asked about placing posters in public places, the Colonel replied:

"You have to remember that we are dealing with two types of public: the law-abiding and the criminal. The criminal public would remove those posters if we attempted to place them."

WHAT THE PUBLIC SAID

The case-writer interviewed four randomly selected members of the public:

Q: What would you do if faced with an emergency, for example, if someone tried to rob you or burgle your property and you needed help?

A: "I would contact my relatives, only those who are mobile and able to help me quickly."

"If someone is breaking into my house, I would contact the police by phoning 10111."

"I will think of a weapon if my life is at stake, alert neighbours by screaming or telephone Flying Squad at 1011."

"I will phone the police at 9111."

Q: Have you ever heard of 10111?

A: All four respondents replied that they had heard of them.

Q: How did you become aware of them?

A: "During the Inkatha / ANC violence, that's when they started operating."

"I saw the number on the yellow police vehicles."

"I saw the number in the telephone directory."

Q: What is 10111 about?

All respondents mentioned handling emergencies and crime prevention.

Q: What do you think are the benefits to the community?

"I would say not that much, but the sound of their sirens makes criminals stop whatever they are doing."

"If you are alone and a burglar comes in, you can phone for help."

"Like all police, they normally arrive very late after they have been called."

"They attend to your problem when called."

Q: Do you think people phone 10111 when there is an emergency?

A: "They may use it, but what about those without telephones – what are they expected to do?"

"Only those with phones."

Q: What would you expect 10111 to do better in the future?

A: "I do not know since I have not used the number."

"They should do what 911 is doing, as we see on TV."

"They should increase the number of personnel in their cars, to be more than two."

Q: Is there a difference between the Flying Squad and the Riot Squad?

A: "There is. Riot Squad responds to riots, while 10111 responds to emergencies, but only when a person has phoned them."

"Yes, there is; if you phone 10111 police come immediately. The Riot Squad does not respond that fast."

"I think they work hand in hand."

"The difference is that it takes seven minutes for 10111 to respond, the Riot Squad takes a longer time."

NON-EMERGENCY CALLS

What is an emergency to one may not be an emergency to another. People have different perceptions and interpretations. The screening and ranking of calls is done internally to distinguish non-emergency from emergency calls. No attempt is made to inform the public about the types of situations in which 10111 should be called.

"We sometimes have to perform the duties of Life Line," said the Colonel. "For example, a man phoned us and said that he was very lonely, his wife had left him and he was about to commit suicide. Luckily for him, we were not busy, and a car was dispatched. The officer chatted with him for a while, and then told him to stop his bloody nonsense. The man was happy to find someone to talk to.

"The chronic problem we have is with people, mainly small kids who telephone and swear at the staff. About 30% of incoming calls are of this type.

"It is not a problem, it is an epidemic. We receive about twenty false calls per day. Unfortunately we have to answer all the calls. I strongly believe that the number should be paid for. High telephone bills would prompt the parents to discipline their kids."

HOW SUCCESS IS MEASURED

Success is measured by the extent to which the system is used by the community, and this has increased tremendously since the unit's inception.

> "You may ask how the public measures the success of my unit. Well, some think it's a bad thing. If it takes us five minutes to attend to a complaint, the complainant is happy, and he tells only two people. If it takes us two hours to respond, the complainant will be angry; he tells everybody, including his priest, that the Flying Squad is useless.
>
> "There has been some positive feedback from the public. For example, there was a case which was attended to by a normal yellow police car. When a 10111 Flying Squad car arrived at the scene, the lady complainant politely asked the police in the yellow car to leave, now that the 'real police' had arrived. I wish we had more feedback from the public we are serving."

THE FUTURE

The system is essentially manually operated. There are plans to install a computerised system to automate the control room, and the handling of (among others):
- incoming calls
- on-line data entry by telephone operators
- monitoring of patrol cars.

Portable cordless radio-microphones will replace the present fixed-position ones.

The case-writer was shown some of the new computer equipment that had arrived but was not yet in use. There are plans to extend and refurbish the present operations room.

> "If you visit the place a year from now, you will find it completely changed," assured the Colonel. He folded his arms. "I restate my case. There can be no New South Africa without us. All governments of the world have a common enemy – crime. Crime can only be combated by an efficient police force. When people are not safe in their homes, in their work places and elsewhere, then there is no future. Without an efficient police system there is no future."

QUESTIONS

1. Sketch the delivery system of Soweto's 10111 service.
2. Evaluate the internal marketing of 10111 in Soweto.
3. Given the information in the case study, how can the marketing of the service be improved? What action(s) could be taken to address public perceptions of the Soweto Flying Squad?
4. Evaluate the management of capacity by Soweto's 10111 service.
5. How can 10111 evaluate its service quality?

6. How can the Soweto service be improved?
7. What are the main problems and issues in this case? How could they be addressed?

APPENDIX 1
SOWETO FLYING SQUAD ORGANISATIONAL CHART

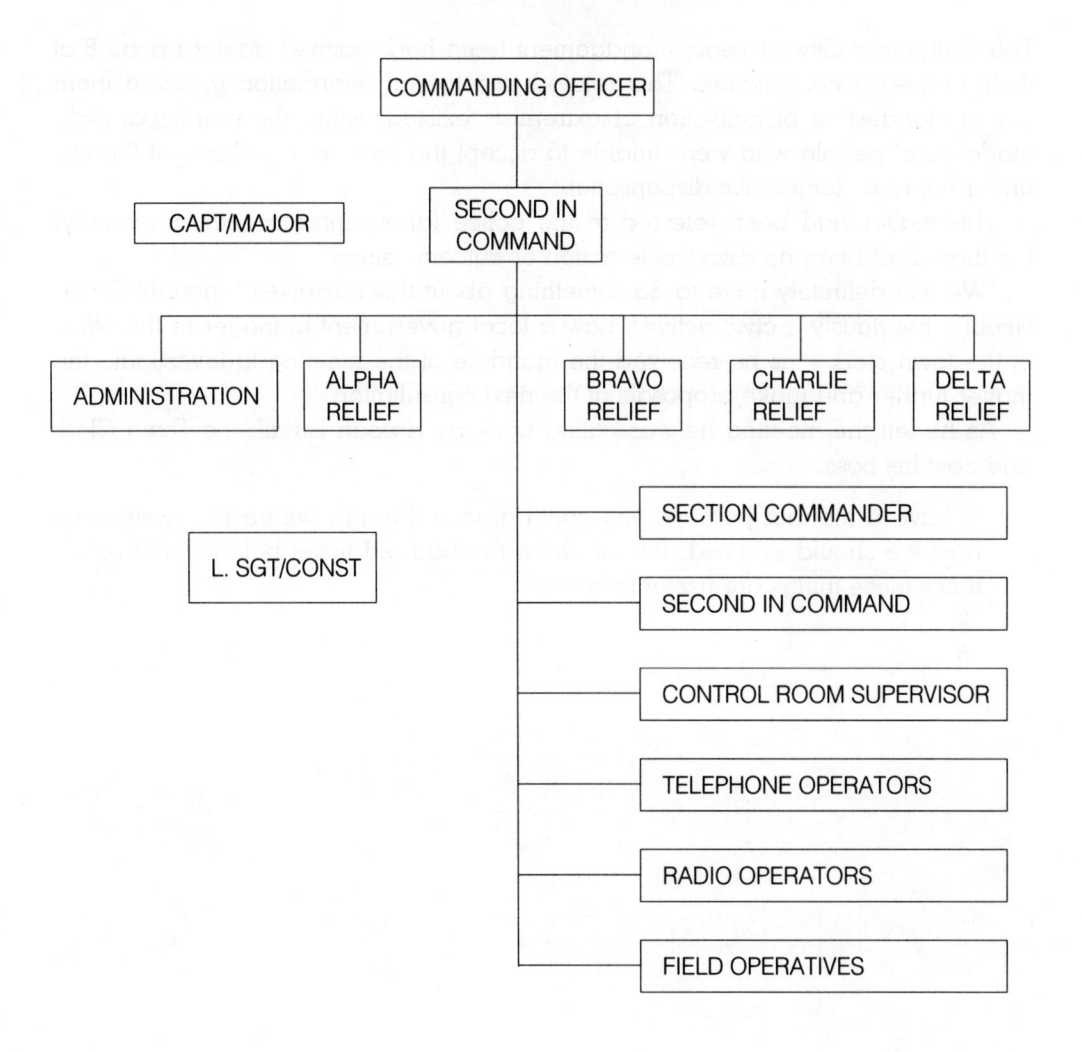

```
                        COMMANDING OFFICER
                                │
              ┌─────────────────┤
              │                 │
         CAPT/MAJOR      SECOND IN COMMAND
                                │
    ┌───────────────┬───────────┼───────────┬───────────┐
    │               │           │           │           │
ADMINISTRATION    ALPHA       BRAVO       CHARLIE     DELTA
                  RELIEF      RELIEF      RELIEF      RELIEF
    │                           │
L. SGT/CONST                    ├── SECTION COMMANDER
                                │
                                ├── SECOND IN COMMAND
                                │
                                ├── CONTROL ROOM SUPERVISOR
                                │
                                ├── TELEPHONE OPERATORS
                                │
                                ├── RADIO OPERATORS
                                │
                                └── FIELD OPERATIVES
```

CASE STUDY NINETEEN

SPIES THAT CAME IN FROM THE COLD

Andries van Rooyen

The Cairncross City strategic management team had reached agenda point 8 at their bi-weekly consultation. This related to informal information given to them that a clandestine organisation of extremists existed within the municipal staff, made up of people who were unable to accept the non-racial policies of the city under the new democratic dispensation.

This matter had been referred to the police (about three months previously) but there had been no discernible action or outcome since.

"We will definitely have to do something about this ourselves," thought Simon Nkobi – previously a civic activist, now a local government manager in the office of the town clerk – as he received the mandate of the meeting to investigate the matter further and make proposals at the next consultation.

As he left the meeting he was called back by Hassan Ismail, the Town Clerk and now his boss.

> "I have a file that perhaps you could glance through before recommending how we should proceed. It's all about the bad old times before – but sometimes these things are useful to know."

THE FILE

DOCUMENT A: A LETTER FROM CHRIS SEEKERS TO COUNCILLOR ENGELS

Chris Seekers
Department of the City Treasurer
Cairncross City Council

Councillor Engels
16 4th Avenue
Highten
23 January 1989

Dear Councillor Engels

During the past year I have received an alarming number of requests from Peter Schonfield to make payments of amounts of R300,00 to 'sources' for services rendered to the Security Division of the Council. Although the request forms always carry the requisite signatures, namely, those of the Chief Executive (Town Clerk), the Director of the Public Safety Department, the Manager of the Security Division, and the Assistant Manager (Monitorial Services) of the Security Division, a number of issues worry me.

Firstly, the identity of these 'sources' is never disclosed to me so I have no way of establishing whether the money is ever paid to the people concerned. Secondly, to the best of my knowledge, the details of these payments are never disclosed to councillors. The particulars pertaining to the services rendered by these 'sources', as detailed on the forms submitted (see attached: Document B), seem to me to be part of spying activities on organisations and therefore also on the people involved in these organisations who, according to my knowledge of politics, are all opponents of the ruling National Party.

Given the frequency with which these requests are coming in, I thought it only right that I make you aware of my concerns.

Yours faithfully

Chris Seekers
Accountant

DOCUMENT B: PAYMENT REQUEST FORM

CITY OF CAIRNCROSS

Security Division
Public Safety Department

1. **PARTICULARS OF SERVICE:** Source is a member of the Transport and General Workers Union (TGWU). He regularly attends and reports on TGWU meetings. Source acts as a recruiting officer for TGWU. Source therefore has contact with student organisations and periodically reports on these organisations.

2. **REMARKS:** The under-mentioned amount is requested as remuneration for the services of the source. The task fulfilled is very dangerous. Due to the departmental placement of the source, it is not possible to remunerate him for work executed outside normal working hours.

3. **RECOMMENDATION:** It is recommended that an amount of R300,00 be paid to the source.

10-1-1989
Date

T. Klue
Asst Manager: Monitorial Services

CERTIFICATE OF THE MANAGER: SECURITY DIVISION

Source is trusted by the Trade Union and is therefore in a position to acquire important information. Payment recommended.

17/1/89
Date

A Rabbitts
Manager

PAYMENT RECOMMENDED

20-1-1989
Date

P. Lombard
Director: Public Safety Department

PAYMENT RECOMMENDED

1989-01-27
Date

K. Kraukamp
Chief Executive/Town Clerk

DOCUMENT C: NOTE TO THE FILE, MARCH 1989

On 24 March 1989, the *Cairncross Herald* published a news report on alleged events which it dubbed "The City Hall Spy Scandal". The report referred to a sinister spy network operating deep within the Cairncross City Council.

The allegations in the report caused an uproar notably at the fact that ratepayers' money had been used to spy on people engaged in peaceful organisational activity. Public indignation was so great that an enquiry seemed imperative.

Councillors, who disclaimed any knowledge of these alleged practices, wanted to know how the operation had been funded, to whom it was accountable, and why the Council had become involved in clandestine activities which, if they had to be done, were a State function. In a statement issued by some seven trade unions representing 20 000 Council employees, it was said:

> "It was with abhorrence that we learn that we are considered to be within the investigative framework and objectives of the Security Division of the Public Safety Department, and that we have been under surveillance since the inception of the information network. We are bitter and disillusioned with the despicable treatment afforded us. The relationship of mutual trust and understanding which existed between us and the City Council has been shattered."

On 29 March 1989, the Cairncross City Council resolved to request the Administrator to appoint a Commission of Enquiry. On 31 March 1989 the Administrator appointed a Commission with the following terms of reference: to enquire into the validity and justification of alleged irregularities in connection with certain security matters in the Security Division of the Public Safety Department of the City Council of Cairncross, as exposed in recent press reports, and to further investigate the question as to whether any violations of any ordinance, regulation, or other act in regard to the safeguarding of the Council's information, in connection with security matters, have occurred.

DOCUMENT D: EXCERPT FROM REPORT OF COMMISSION OF ENQUIRY

In October 1983 a retired policeman, Allen Rabbitts, joined the municipal service of Cairncross. On 1 November 1985 Rabbitts was transferred to the Security Division and he was soon promoted as manager of this division.

Every sizeable local authority, including Cairncross, has a security division to safeguard council buildings and property. The *National Key Points Act,* 1980, created important duties for the local authority. There were six key points, in the Cairncross area guarded by access control, electronic fencing and radio connection to control posts. Regular inspection was done to ensure that the guards there were at the ready. There were also places called Important Places and Buildings (IPBs) which were guarded around the clock, but less intensively than the National Key Points (NKPs). Electrical substations and even parks and reserves were also guarded.

On assuming his duties in the Security Division, Rabbitts found that there was co-operation with the Defence Force but, in his view, inadequate linkage with National Intelligence and the Bureau of Information. During the course of 1985 a disquieting increase in unrest and violence had occurred in South Africa and there was a mushrooming of organisations who were against apartheid and worked assiduously at propaganda. If this was to be the background against which the coming municipal elections scheduled for 1988 were to take place, the time seemed ripe to Rabbitts for improving security services.

Councillor Jim Davies, Chair of the Executive Committee of Cairncross City Council, was a staunch and active supporter of the ruling National Party which also held the majority of seats in the Cairncross City Council. It was no secret that Davies aspired to becoming a Member of Parliament and that he left no stone unturned to promote his candidature. He knew that his position as Chair of the Executive Committee promoted his influence in circles that mattered.

Jim Davies was, however, also deeply worried about the steady increase in criticism of and resistance to the policies of his party, which manifested in sporadic but continuous violence. He agreed with his party's viewpoint that this was part of the "revolutionary onslaught" which was Communist-inspired and propagated by followers of the underground movement of the banned African National Congress and South African Communist Party and its sympathisers. Jim's concerns were confirmed by an intelligence evaluation of the Security Division of Council pertaining to the revolutionary onslaught on Cairncross City Council. The report convinced him that something had to be done, although he was not sure what or how. From experience, he knew that the matter was of a sensitive political nature in that not all councillors and officials agreed with the viewpoint of the National Party on the "total onslaught".

Reflecting on what should be done, Jim decided that he should discuss the matter with his fellow-Councillor Dick Krick (Deputy Chairman of the Executive Committee), Karl Kraukamp, the Chief Executive/Town Clerk, Paul Lombaard, the Director of the Public Safety Department and Allen Rabbitts, the Manager of the Security Division, because he knew that they were also supporters of the National Party

The opportunity for Jim Davies to voice his concerns arose soon enough when Allen Rabbitts delivered a lecture on security at a meeting for departmental heads convened by the Town Clerk. It was attended by Councillor Jim Davies, the Town Clerk, and Paul Lombaard, Director of the Public Safety Department. After the lecture, there was an informal discussion between the aforementioned foursome in which Rabbitts mentioned the topic of informers or spies, who were to be called 'sources'. He pointed out that 'sources' are employed world wide in security and police forces and are widely recognised in technical literature. Councillor Davies agreed that 'sources' should be appointed to gather information for reward, on organisations identified as part of the 'total onslaught' and after discussion, Davies, Kraukamp, Lombaard and Rabbitts decided to introduce this system. In their opinion the 'mandate' for this operation was contained in a Council resolution of 29 November 1983 which provided for the delivery of an effective monitoring service as reflected in the purpose and functions of the Security Division. Payment could be made under the Chief Executive's delegated authority, granted to him by Council, to spend amounts of up to R300 without special permission from the Management Committee. The decision taken by the four was formalised when the Management Committee took the following resolution on the recommendation of Kraukamp:

> SPECIAL SECURITY COMMITTEE
> The Chief Executive advised the Committee that in his opinion it would be desirable for a small committee to be created to deal specifically with matters affecting the security of the Council and its officials before such items were discussed by the Management Committee.
>
> RESOLVED
> That a special security committee, consisting of the Chairman of the Management Committee, the Chief Executive, the Director of the Public Safety Department and the Manager of the Security Division, be appointed to consider all security aspects of the Council, through which all recommendations concerning expenditure on security shall be channelled in the first instance and reported to the Management Committee.

Rabbitts instructed Tom Klue, the Assistant Manager (Monitorial Services) of the Security Division of the Public Safety Department to recruit "sources". Klue was chosen because he had security experience from his earlier sojourn in the Defence Force. The strictest secrecy was maintained. The "sources" did not know each other and in documentation they were only referred to by code number. In the hierarchy below Klue, were "handlers" in charge of the "sources". The "sources" would report to the "handlers" and the "handlers" to Klue. From him the information went to the processing section. Jim Davies also received a copy of the reports at his own request. Payment of "sources" was done by the "handlers", after approval by Klue, Rabbitts, Lombaard and ultimately Kraukamp.

By means of the assistance of "sources" the Security Division was able to compile profiles on organisations, public figures, political leaders, councillors and fellow-officials, who were identified for investigation.

The Council's legal advisers were never consulted on this matter and at no stage was written legal advice obtained on the idea of "sources". Allen Rabbitts stated that he had obtained assurances from Kraukamp that there was statutory empowerment for the scheme.

In fact, there is provision for a measure of secrecy in municipal affairs. An example is to be found in section 57 of the *Local Government (Administration and Elections) Ordinance*, 1960, of Transvaal, which *inter alia* reads:

(5) A management committee may, of its own accord or by direction of the council, take steps which are within the power of the council for the protection of the personnel or the property of the council or property under the control of the council against attacks or sabotage and steps so taken shall be deemed to have been taken by the council.

(7) Notwithstanding any provision to the contrary contained in this or any other Ordinance –
   (a) the minutes of the proceedings of the management committee regarding any steps contemplated in subsection (5) shall be recorded separately from the minutes of its other proceedings and kept in a separate minute book by and in the custody of the town secretary;
   (b) the management committee shall not report to the council regarding any steps taken in terms of subsection (5) and the minutes of its proceedings in connection therewith shall not be tabled at a meeting of the council;
   (c) any question regarding the steps contemplated in subsection (5) shall not be referred to the council for decision; and
   (d) the steps contemplated in subsection (5) and the proceedings of the management committee in connection therewith shall not be discussed or referred to at a meeting of the council: provided that a councillor may, subject to such conditions as the council may impose, inspect, during ordinary office hours, the minute book referred to in paragraph (a).

(8) No person shall, either directly or indirectly, publish or disclose any information regarding the steps contemplated in subsection (5) or regarding the proceedings of the management committee in connection therewith.

DOCUMENT E: NOTE FROM THE COMMISSION OF ENQUIRY ON THE LEGAL CONTEXT

Undercover agents of the Security Division of the Public Safety Department monitored and infiltrated trade unions and various voluntary associations. They reported on confidential proceedings as well as on the private affairs and movements of individuals.

The gathering of information was done by pretending to be interested in the organisation and by winning the trust and confidence of the office bearers. Information so gained was reported to superior officers and sifted by the processing section and also passed on to Military Intelligence; there was close co-operation with the military.

Conduct of this nature is universally accepted as a matter of course in military intelligence in times of peace as well as in war. The same applies to the police force. These bodies are, however, specially covered in this regard by legislation. The statutory matrix against which the Public Safety Department was working is as follows:

- Subsections 57(5), (7) and (8) of the *Transvaal Local Government (Administration and Elections) Ordinance*, 1960.
- The *National Key Points Act*, 1980. There were six such key points in the Cairncross area and by reason of the definition of 'owner', the Town Clerk/Chief Executive was made responsible in terms of section 3 of the Act for safeguarding them. Under section 3(1) of the *National Key Points Act*, 1980, the owner of a national key point "shall after consultation with the Minister (of Defence) at his own expense take steps to the satisfaction of the Minister in respect of the security of the said key point". The section firstly envisages that the owner would take only such steps as were determined in consultation with the Minister of Defence. The section must secondly be construed according to the ordinary canons of construction to direct that lawful steps be taken. The purpose of the section is to burden the owner of a key point with certain duties.
- Under section 2(1) of the *Control of Access to Public Premises and Vehicles Act*, 1985, the owner of any public premise or any public vehicle may "take such steps as he may consider necessary for the safeguarding of those premises or that vehicle and the contents thereof, as well as for the protection of the people therein or thereon". The section is concerned with 'public premises' (defined *inter alia* as premises "to which a member of the public has a right of access, or is usually admitted or to which he may be admitted") and 'public vehicles' (defined *inter alia* as vehicles "used for the transport ... of members of the public"). The purpose of the section is merely to permit the owner to impinge upon the public's rights of access to and use of those premises and vehicles to safeguard them.
- The Chief Executive (Town Clerk) was appointed by the Administrator as head of civil defence in terms of section 4(2) of the Transvaal *Civil Defence Ordinance*, 1977. In that connection he was urged to organise matters in such a way that control could be exercised in cases of disaster.
- The mandate contained in a Council resolution of 29 November 1983. This was not a statutory provision, but had the same effect.

Invasion of privacy is both a criminal and civil wrong. The offence of *crimen injuria* is appropriate to the facts. *Crimen injuria* is defined as:

> "unlawfully, intentionally and seriously impairing the *dignitas* of another" (Hunt, *S A Criminal Law and Procedure II*. 2nd ed. p.525).

It is important to bear in mind that our courts use the prevailing *boni mores* in this context as a benchmark to distinguish between permissible and impermissible intrusions upon the privacy of others. In S v A 1971 (2) SA 293 (T) Botha A J said at 299 C that the court "must give effect to what it conceives to be the prevailing *boni mores* in accordance with public opinion".

The following passage from Flemming, *Law of Torts,* 7th ed., p.572 is relevant:

> "No simple answer can be given to the question to what extent contemporary law affords protection for what is often compendiously called the 'right of privacy'. In its broadest sense, the interest involved is that of 'being left alone', of sheltering one's private life from the degrading effect of intrusion or exposure to public view. Demand for legal protection of this interest appears only in a relatively advanced state of civilisation, with increasing refinement in the social and aesthetic values of the community. It becomes more insistent as the intensity of modern life renders desirable some retreat from the world and as personal modesty, dignity and self-respect are increasingly exposed to practices which overstep the bounds of propriety."

It is very likely that in our society a variety of people would argue that spying is justifiable in all places where public safety is at stake. In this respect it is useful to look at what Parliament has done.

Parliament has recognised that activities of this kind would ordinarily be unlawful and has consequently expressly legislated to permit certain departments of state to engage in the covert collection, evaluation, correlation and interpretation of intelligence. It did so in section 3(1) of the *Security Intelligence and State Security Council Act,* 1972, which provides as follows:

> "Where any law expressly or by implication requires any department of State, other than the Bureau [that is, the Bureau for State Security], to perform any function with reference to the security of the Republic or the combating of any threat to the security of the Republic, such law shall be deemed to empower such department to collect departmental intelligence (that is, "information which relates to any function concerning the security of the Republic which by any law has been assigned to a department of State") and to evaluate, correlate and interpret intelligence for the purpose of discharging such function: Provided that such a department of State, other than the South African Defence Force in time of war – as defined in section 1 of the *Defence Act,* 1957 (Act No 44 of 1957) – or when discharging counter-intelligence responsibilities entrusted to its military intelligence section, and other than a police force established under any Act of Parliament, when a member of such a last-mentioned force is investigating any offence relating to the security of the Republic or is performing any other function relating to the security of the Republic, shall not collect departmental intelligence within the Republic in a covert manner: Provided ...".

The following features of this provision are germane to this context:

- Only departments of State required by law to perform functions with reference to the security of the Republic or the combating of threats to the security of the Republic are authorised to collect intelligence at all.
- The departments of State so authorised to collect intelligence may, as a rule, not do so in a covert manner. Only the South African Police and the South African Defence Force engage in the covert collection of intelligence, and then only in the circumstances described above, that is, in time of war and when engaged in counter-intelligence.

DOCUMENT F: PUBLIC SAFETY DEPARTMENT: PURPOSE & FUNCTION

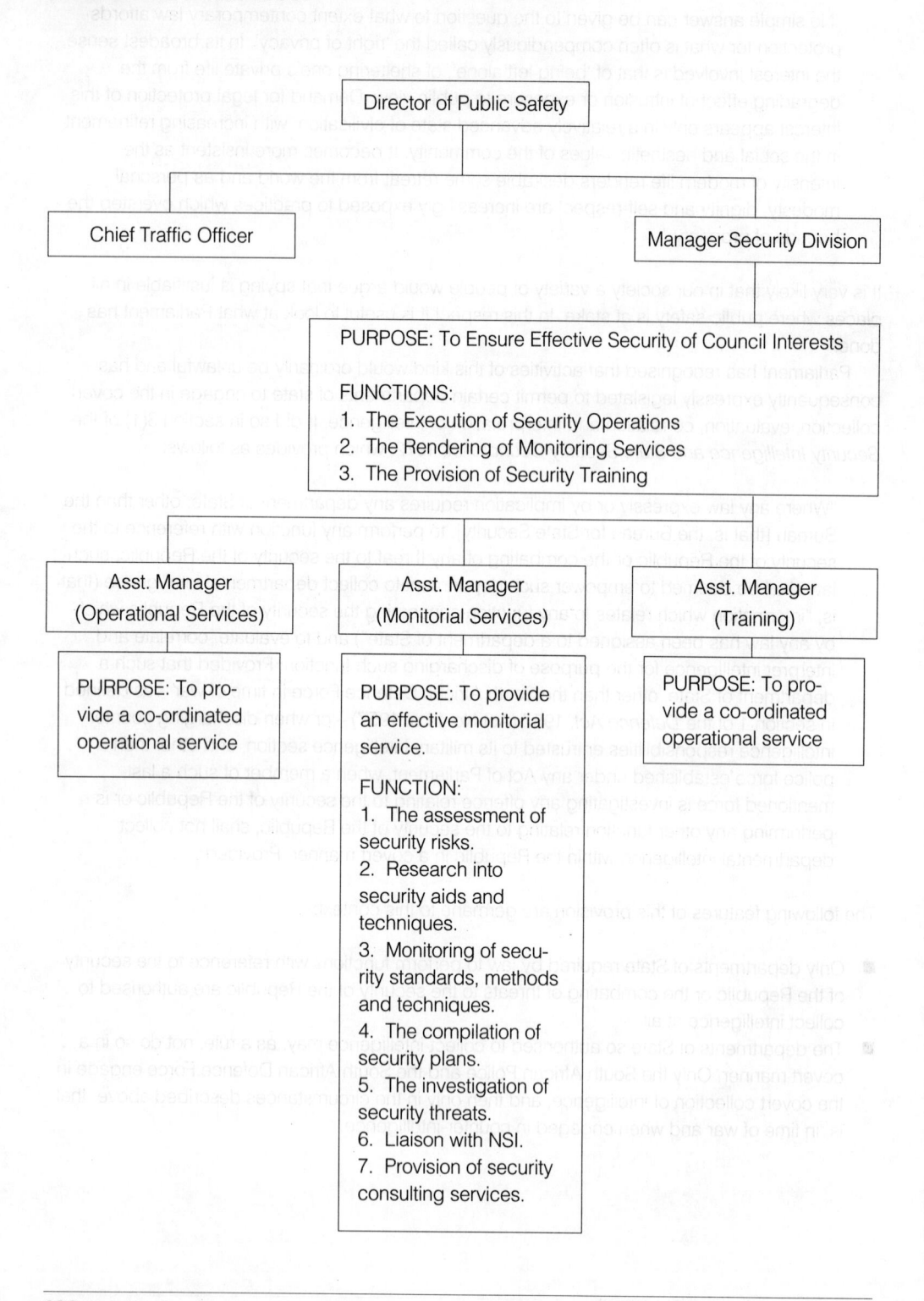

```
                    Director of Public Safety
                    /                        \
       Chief Traffic Officer          Manager Security Division
```

PURPOSE: To Ensure Effective Security of Council Interests

FUNCTIONS:
1. The Execution of Security Operations
2. The Rendering of Monitoring Services
3. The Provision of Security Training

```
   Asst. Manager           Asst. Manager           Asst. Manager
 (Operational Services)   (Monitorial Services)      (Training)
```

PURPOSE: To provide a co-ordinated operational service

PURPOSE: To provide an effective monitorial service.

FUNCTION:
1. The assessment of security risks.
2. Research into security aids and techniques.
3. Monitoring of security standards, methods and techniques.
4. The compilation of security plans.
5. The investigation of security threats.
6. Liaison with NSI.
7. Provision of security consulting services.

PURPOSE: To provide a co-ordinated operational service

DOCUMENT G: EXCERPT FROM REPORT SUBMITTED BY ALLEN RABBITTS TO CAIRNCROSS MANAGEMENT COMMITTEE, DECEMBER 1985

CONFIDENTIAL

INTELLIGENCE EVALUATION: The Revolutionary onslaught on the Cairncross City Council

1 INTRODUCTION

The intensification of the revolutionary onslaught against the government of the Republic of South Africa over the past decade is well known. Due to the nature of the revolutionary onslaught all government institutions which make possible the maintenance of the *status quo* are threatened. The revolutionaries also regard the Cairncross City Council as an extension of government. The City Council is therefore directly and indirectly threatened by the revolutionary onslaught.

15 RECOMMENDATION

It is clear from the aforementioned that the revolutionary onslaught against Cairncross City Council comprises a variety of components. The responsibility of Council towards the Cairncross community requires that steps should be taken against the revolutionary onslaught.

The politicisation, organisation and mobilisation of the mass by revolutionaries is also occurring in the Cairncross community. The strengthening of revolutionary power and the development of alternative structures constitute a real danger to the activities of Council.

In order to combat the revolutionary onslaught successfully it is necessary for Council to co-operate with the security forces of the country. Council should, however, develop its own capacity to cope with this onslaught. This own capacity will of necessity include the development and expansion of an intelligence and counter-intelligence ability.

An efficient and effective intelligence and counter-intelligence system will ensure proactive Council steps due to the foresight provided by the said system. Development of this capacity is required, as matters which affect Council directly might not necessarily be seen as a priority by the security forces at higher government levels.

SIMON NKOBI

Simon Nkobi had to smile. The last document echoed his own feelings in a funny way. He had little confidence in the police to deal with the current security matter and had been prepared to suggest an internal operation by the city security division. Clearly, however, the historical precedent contained some interesting lessons. He was less sure of what line of action to recommend.

CASE STUDY TWENTY

POLICING IN RIETSPRUIT

Etienne Marais

Joe Langa peered rather aimlessly at his wall in his new office at the Area Headquarters, Rietspruit. He had just had a meeting with the Area Commissioner which had been far from satisfactory. The Area Commissioner seemed to think that nothing was really needed in terms of the change management process. "Everything is going really well in this area – we have no problems," he had said.

Only two weeks previously, Mr Joe Langa had been appointed as a member of the National Change Management Task Team. The team had been established by the National Minister of Safety and Security in Order in response to concern about the lack of change in the police force.

Rietspruit had been identified as one of five areas where a pilot "change management" project should be set up. His brief was to establish a process to facilitate change in the area. If the process proved successful, it would be used as the basis of a nationwide change management project.

A key problem facing the project was that the newly formed National Association of Police Officers has been campaigning vigorously against the change management programme. This group involves largely white officers and is opposed to affirmative action as well as changes involving rank structures and the police regulations around the use of firearms. The National Ministry is particularly anxious not to antagonise this group, as this could have a very negative effect both on police command and on the fight against crime, which is a critical national issue.

THE RIETSPRUIT POLICE FORCE

Rietspruit police "area" is centred on the town of Bothasville, which has a police strength of 350. This force is also responsible for policing in the neighbouring township area – known as Gemsbokspruit. The population of Gemsbokspruit is about 70 000 – twice that of Bothasville itself. The main police station, where 260 police are deployed, is in the centre of Bothasville. A second, smaller police station is situated on the outskirts of Gemsbokspruit.

The major policing problem in the area is the existence of five gangs in Gemsbokspruit which have raped and harassed residents. The police have been unable to make progress in prosecuting the gangs, largely because of unwillingness among residents to assist investigators or to appear in court.

Last year 17 people were shot and killed by police staff in the area, 15 of whom were "attempting to avoid arrest". In 14 of the cases the persons were suspects in burglary cases.

MANAGEMENT AND COMMAND

The district is managed through a management committee, which includes heads of all the units, the Area Commissioner and his deputy; as well as the Public Relations Officer. A recent meeting spent 45 minutes discussing action to be taken against 9 people who had been caught drunk on duty at the Gemsbokspruit police station.

Within the management committee, decision making is fairly participative but it is not clear how far this participation extends. Whilst the Area Commissioner asserts that all relevant commanders and units, the most important of which is obviously the Crime Intelligence Service (formerly the SB) are consulted, some people within the force claim that the management committee is a "clique" and that former members of the security branch are "informally involved" in its decision making. Recently the management committee attempted to address the problem of gangs by supplementing the police personnel at the Gemsbok station, the detectives assigned to the task seemed to lack motivation.

ISU – INTERNAL STABILITY UNIT

A unit of the ISU is based in Bothasville and has been deployed in Gemsbokspruit where its members patrol with Casspirs. Although the ISU commander sits on the management committee, he is actually under the command of the National Police Service, based in Pretoria. Within the community, there is widespread dissatisfaction regarding the role of the ISU. Suggestions from the community liaison forum that they should discard R4 rifles have the support of the community policing officers, but have been rejected by the National Command.

POLICE-COMMUNITY RELATIONS

The SAPS has recently established a division of "community policing", and Rietspruit now has two community policing officers whose task it is to liaise with the community and promote the development of a partnership between police and community. In Rietspruit the community policing officer, a Colonel du Preez, works most closely with members of the Crime Intelligence Service (formerly the security branch).

A police-community forum exists, but involves more groups from Bothasville than from the township area. A strong civic organisation is willing to co-operate on the issue of the gangs. It has wider credibility, but has not attended police-community forums because of the failure to deal with certain recommendations regarding the ISU. In part, this is related to the different approaches of the Public Relations officer and the new Community Policing Officer. In particular the PR believes in persuading the community of the need to work with the police, and is angry with the civic for not attending the last meeting. The Community Policing officer wants to go more slowly and consult each organisation individually. He is frustrated because of the way the PR has "lectured" community groups at the meetings, as well as the insistence of the station commander on arresting people for drinking in public. This policy was reinforced when a prominent politician complained of drunk people "loitering" outside his house.

A major concern from the community side is that of victim treatment – the way in which police deal with, in particular, victims of domestic violence or rape. The National Training Board has not yet accredited a course which would give police officers appropriate training and local NGOs, although willing to contribute their expertise in this type of training, are unable to do so because their programmes would not be accredited for at least a year.

The Area Commissioner, Colonel Freek Kleynhans sees the police-community forum as important, but sometimes blocks recommendations which arise from the forum. The community recently suggested that guards at the police station should not be armed with shotguns, but Freek talks of a previous experience where his police station was attacked.

STRATEGIC PLANNING

Members of the Corporate Planning division of Head Office have also visited the region to discuss the strategic plan for the year. The local district is tasked with working on it's own strategic plan as well, but has not given input to the national plan. The national plan is due to be published within 10 days.

Key elements of the strategic plan which was presented by head office are:
- The establishment of a strategy of community policing, where the thrust is towards the fostering of greater police-community co-operation. In particular this includes: The development of police-community liaison structures into workable forums for consultation and feedback about community needs in terms of policing. It also includes making the uniform police more visible and accessible through the establishment of satellite police stations and increased use of foot, bicycle and horse patrols.
- Continued decentralisation of a variety of functions at provincial and area level, in order that local police commissioners have more autonomy and flexibility to adapt to local needs. This strategy dates back over a period of eight months and is in keeping with the new Police Service Act which provides for a twin track promotions policy to allow (mainly black) officers without the necessary academic qualifications to be promoted on the basis of a competency test.

PROBLEMS RAISED BY BLACK MEMBERS OF THE FORCE

Black members, who constitute 43% of the force, are not part of decision making. The strategic planning process, for example, involved only the heads of the various units – all of whom are white. There is also a problem with language – most black members in this area speak only English, yet monthly briefing sessions (involving all police in the district) are conducted predominantly in Afrikaans.

Community concerns about the role of the ISU are shared by black members of the force. Some of them say the ISU is arrogant and racist. It has also been said that the ISU units are reluctant to get involved in "non-unrest" incidents because of the amount of time unit members would spend in court, should even a small proportion of the cases encountered come to court. This means that they tend to be unresponsive when called on to intervene in cases of domestic violence, intimidation by gang members and so called "petty crime".

The focus of black police personnel's dissatisfaction is the Gemsbokspruit station. In essence a former "municipal police" unit, it is clear that the station is not being properly utilised, mainly because of the attitude of officers in Bothasville, who say that the station is "useless". It is true that the personnel there are not well trained and there are disciplinary problems which include drunkenness in the station. Assaults on suspects have been reported. However there are several members of the unit who have impressed their Bothasville colleagues with their professional behaviour. Unfortunately, the Area Commissioner seems to have deliberately undermined them, and the CID has on a number of occasions ignored their suggestions regarding the gang issue and the community protection role that the Gemsbokspruit Unit could play.

Black police in Bothasville see the problem as one of racial discrimination.

EXERCISE

1. Identify what needs to change in Rietspruit. What is the ideal situation for the policing of the district?
2. What are the factors resisting change that Joe Langa has to deal with, if he is to be effective?
3. Develop a plan of action for Joe Langa: what should he do to change the police organisation in Rietspruit?

CASE STUDY TWENTY-ONE

LIFE IS TOO SHORT TO DRINK BAD WINE: THE THORNY PROBLEM OF CHARDONNAY THAT TURNED OUT TO BE AUXERROIS

Erwin Schwella

The following apology was published in three newspapers during the second half of 1987:

KLIPSIG
DISTRIK ASHTON

APOLOGIE

Ek, Johan Potgieter, bied hiermee my onvoorwaardelike apologie aan teenoor Mnr Piet Nel van Druiwepan, vir foutiewelike beweringe wat ek aangaande hom gemaak het voor die Klopper-kommissie gedurende Januarie 1986. Ek trek hiermee die onderhawige beweringe onvoorwaardelik terug.

Geteken te Kaapstad op hierdie 14de Augustus, 1987.

J Potgieter   JOHAN POTGIETER

TRANSLATION

I, Johan Potgieter, hereby offer my unconditional apology to Mr Piet Nel of Druiwepan, for false allegations that I made regarding him, before the Klopper commission during January 1986. I hereby retract the above allegations unconditionally.

Signed in Cape Town on this 14 August, 1987.

J Potgieter

This apology, from one prominent Cape wine farmer, Johan Potgieter of Klipsig, to another, Mr Piet Nel of Druiwepan, was the final curtain on a drama that had unfolded over a period of approximately 10 years. This drama involved a number of Cape wine farmers, some of the large wine companies, the state bureaucracy and the Klopper commission mentioned in the apology.

It had involved incidents that had had the potential to do as much damage to the South African wine industry as the adding of anti-freeze to Austrian wines had done to the wine industry of Austria.

BACKGROUND

The scene is the annual "boeredag" (farmers' day) at Elsenburg. The air is filled with the aroma of braaivleis (barbecued meat) and the speeches having just come to an end, everybody is looking forward to the more relaxed part of the day. Underneath the oak trees, tables are set with salads, vegetables and other culinary delights. The fine wines of the region are being served and the mood is genial and improving as people, aided by the good wine, interact socially.

Koos van der Walt of Rietboom is in deep discussion with a number of wine farmers. "It is a disgrace that we have to try and make quality wines while being hamstrung by international sanctions," he says, "but it is even worse that our own bureaucracy adds to our problems. It is important that we remain competitive internationally yet these bureaucrats set up red tape that results in delays of from five to ten years before we can obtain necessary plant material. We all know that good wines are born in the vineyard. I think that we should make our own plans to get the necessary material. Presently the worldwide trend is towards the versatility of wines made from cultivars such as chardonnay. Our official procedures are such, though, that local production through the KWV [The Co-operative Wine Growers Association] does not succeed in coming to light with quality vines. The process for importation of such material is so lengthy that it is just not worthwhile ..." Other farmers join in the debate and generally agree with his views.

A THORNY PROBLEM

On leaving, Koos is followed by one of the people in the group who has listened attentively but said very little. As soon as they are out of earshot of the other farmers the man calls out, "Koos, I can't agree more with what you said about our problems with the bureaucrats. We at Percy's Fruit Farms are being stifled by the bureaucracy but have decided to make a plan to bypass the whole bureaucratic rigmarole and to import directly." Koos feels nervous and starts to walk on "Yes, we know it is dangerous and possibly even illegal," says the man, "but we cannot possibly do business with so much red tape smothering us."

Koos stops in his tracks, and more conversation ensues. After a while he has to agree. "If that is the only way then I would also like to get hold of some of the material by bypassing the bureaucracy!" he says. On that note, the two men nod their heads and shake hands.

Subsequent discussions and decisions probably led to numerous attempts by many other parties, some more successful than others, to import vine materials illegally. The extent and results of these imports caused a shock to the industry during 1985 when it was made public that many of the vines imported were not, as had been believed, the noble chardonnay but less highly regarded auxerrois vines. At the time it not only created embarrassment for the farmers but led to further allegations of serious shortcomings on the side of the government institutions involved. Two quotes from newspaper reports during 1985 substantiate these concerns:

Beeld wrote on 1 May 1985: "The vine planting season is upon us. Many more spurious chardonnay vines may be planted this winter. Wine farmers are very upset. Rumours are going around to the effect that up to 60 000 vines have been smuggled into the country and planted. Yet more serious is the fact that vineyard pests may enter the country."

Die Burger quoted Piet Nel of Druiwepan on 1 May 1985 as having said: "I cannot believe the Department of Agriculture has, for a considerable time, been unaware of the doubts regarding the cultivar purity of the material. It has been the subject of discussion amongst farmers and vine growers for at least two years. I know the illegal importation of grafted vines from abroad was brought explicitly to the attention of senior officials of the Department last year and that nothing was done about it. I would like to see a proper inquiry instituted into the whole affair, to ensure that such a thing, which poses so great a threat to the entire wine industry, will never happen again."

Tensions were building up as fingers were pointed in all directions, and Mr Nel featured prominently during this time. To get to the bottom of the rumours, a Commission of Inquiry was appointed. The announcement was made in the *Financial Mail* of 29 November 1985:

WINE SCANDAL:
State Probe On The Way

The intrigue of Falcon Crest could pale in comparison. The State President has appointed a one-man commission into SA's great chardonnay wine scandal and, if the rumblings in the vineyards are anything to go by, his investigation will be a source of national controversy for months to come.

The announcement in last Friday's *Government Gazette* of the commission headed by Christiaan Klopper caught the wine industry unawares, but *FM* inquiries indicate its work is essential if SA is to be spared serious damage to its reputation as a quality producer of authentic wines.

Klopper's brief is to delve into the complex world of chardonnay vines (source of the jewel of white wines), as well as orlaz riesling, pinot gris, and auxerrois vines. He is to determine who imported them; where they came from; how it was pulled off; whether import regulations were evaded; where the vines are now; and whether anyone is illicitly breeding from the uncertified vines. In short, what is going on down on the estates?

Cynics chide that only someone with a good nose for wine will be up to the task. Klopper, who retired as president of the regional court in the northern Transvaal in 1982, admits to an interest in the subject, but says he is no expert.

The commission has its roots in an acutely embarrassing problem for the South African wine industry which is threatening to assume proportions akin to Austria's anti-freeze scandal. A great proportion of the Cape's chardonnay vine clones may not be chardonnay at all, but a similar variety called auxerrois which was allegedly "smuggled" into the country about seven years ago.

If this is so, the identity of all wines classed as

chardonnay by the Wine and Spirit Board would obviously be in doubt. Similar anomalies exist in the classification of other cultivars, according to the wine men.

"We need to get to the bottom of this since it is a matter of conjecture as to what is really happening," maintains Piet Nel, patriarch of the Nel family who own the Druiwepan estate. Nel is also chairman of the Western Cape Agricultural Union which has allegedly implicated the Nurseryman's Association among its affiliates. The nurseries, along with the KWV, dispense cuttings to the farmers.

Nel believes Klopper faces a big task. However, there is apparently no great problem in identifying the chardonnay vine. It is highly distinctive, Nel says, and the leaf could not be missed by anybody who knows what to look for. Unfortunately, the early 'official' clones, those tested and approved by government's standards safeguard – the Nietvoorbij Viticultural and Oenological Research Institute in Stellenbosch – have evidently earned a reputation as temperamental vineyard disasters riddled with leafroll virus.

New chardonnay clones recently approved by Nietvoorbij will not be available from the KWV for a couple of years. It appears possible that some farmers couldn't wait. Desperate to get onto the chardonnay bandwagon, they are said to have attempted to get cuttings any way they could, literally bringing them in from Europe under raincoats and bypassing usual checks.

Vineyards cost some R20 000/ha to establish and it then takes five to six years to bring wine onto the market. Damages to farmers could run into millions if chardonnay and other plantings are proved to be phoney.

Still, this would be peanuts compared to the damage implicit in a loss of reputation by South African wines in general.

It all comes down to a monumental headache for Wine and Spirits Board chairman Jacob Deist, who is charged with administering the cultivar and wine of origin system. Deist could not be reached as the *FM* went to press.

Klopper intends to conduct his investigation into the alleged scandal in public from the Stellenbosch magistrate's court. Hearings are due to begin mid-January.

The appointed commission, referred to as the Klopper Commission, started its inquiry during November 1985, but its own functioning was not without controversy, as its activities dragged on for nearly two years. The report was finally tabled in August 1987. In Business Day of 8 July 1987, it was alleged that:

> "The main reaction in and around Parliament at the moment is an activity called 'hide the report'. The function of this time-honoured game is to delay as long as possible – and hopefully forever – the general distribution of bad news. The latest report to 'vanish' is the Klopper Commission's investigation of the illegal importation of vineyard material – in other words the chardonnay scandal."

When the report was finally tabled, it contained a couple of ironic surprises. It found that the following people were involved in the unlawful importation and receipt of material:

- Dr Julius de Abreu who initiated imports while still employed by a government institute, the Viticultural and Oenological Research Institute (VORI).
- Mr Peter Richardson of Richardson's Vineyards;
- Percy's Fruit Farms;
- Mr Paul Smit of Paulshof;
- Mr Piet Nel of Druiwepan; and
- Mr Johan Potgieter of Klipsig.

It was during the hearings of the commission that Mr Johan Potgieter stated that he was surprised that Mr Piet Nel had pushed for a commission of inquiry and had loudly announced that he had destroyed all auxerrois, while the vines still flourished at Druiwepan. For these statements he later had to apologise publicly.

Although the commission referred the possibility of criminal action to the Attorney-General, it also stated that the imports were subject to certain mitigating circumstances. These were:

- The illegal importers were honest with the commission before, during and after the investigation.
- The illegal imports had at the time of the report not been associated with any vine diseases. (The primary objective of the permit system and state involvement was to prevent vine diseases and pests.)
- The laxity of the authorities with regard to illegal imports, as they seemed to have let imports continue even after they had become aware of them.
- The illegal imports expanded the country's wine spectrum.
- The procedure for the importation of new cultivars was too cumbersome:

(1) From 1971 onwards an application had first to be approved by the Co-ordinating Committee for the evaluation of Wine Grape Cultivars, known as the Cultivar Committee. After favourable evaluation of the application it was sent to –
(2) the Plant Introduction Officer for the issue of a permit in terms of section 3 of the Agricultural Pests Act.
(3) The import permit was then sent to the foreign supplier. Material was then sent directly to –
(4) the Plant Quarantine Station at Stellenbosch. Here the plants were tested for foreign diseases and basically held under quarantine for two years. If the Plant Quarantine Station was satisfied that the material was acceptable phytosanitarily the material was supplied to –
(5) the VORI for viticultural and oenological evaluation. Their evaluation took at least three years. If the material was then certified phytosanitarily satisfactory and cultivar pure the material was handed to –
(6) the KWV with the certificate for multiplication. The KWV then established the material in foundation blocks and mother blocks. Only then was the material given to the breeder and could the farmer obtain material for establishment on his land.

In giving evidence before the commission, Distillers' Corporation stated that it was not uncommon for wine to be produced only 20 to 27 years after a new cultivar had first been imported. According to the commission it was clear that, in the past, wine farmers had been unnecessarily hampered by red tape in importing new cultivars.

The commission recommended new procedures to alleviate the problems faced by importers, including a shortening of the time required for importation. In its final paragraph the commission stated that it had been told that the word chardonnay was of French origin and that it meant thistle. A thistle is always thorny and consequently difficult to handle. The commission had certainly found the chardonnay grape a thorny problem that had had to be handled carefully and, at times, with gloves.

Despite the recommendations of the commission, debate continued to rage within the wine industry. In the many gatherings that followed, wine farmers asked themselves a number of questions such as:

- is the state justified in attempting to control imports in such circumstances and what is the basis for the involvement of the state?
- if state intervention is necessary, which parties should be involved and what should the nature of such involvement be?
- how can the process of policy-making and public management provide access for the input of various interest groups in this situation?
- are citizens justified in acting independently if they feel that their own and even national interests are detrimentally affected by inefficient and cumbersome state intervention?

CASE STUDY TWENTY-TWO

TOWARDS A POLICY ON HAWKING: A ROLE-PLAY EXERCISE

Mark Swilling

The inner-city areas of many of the main cities and large towns in the PWV Province are being choked up by hawkers. A recent report estimated that there were about 100 000 hawkers selling their goods in these areas.

Tensions are rising. Black and white shop owners, whose businesses are suffering, have begun to mobilise and have formed the Shop Owners' Association to take up the issue and to lobby the Minister. The Chairperson of the Shop Owners' Association is Bruce Hanson.

The hawkers are organised into the Hawkers' Association. They argue that the high levels of unemployment in the country, force them to engage in hawking activities. They are completely opposed to any changes in the existing arrangement, as they feel that if they are all forced into a single area, they will lose money because they will not have access to the pedestrians walking along the pavement. The Hawkers' Association is led by **Mr Phaliso.**

Ordinary working people have begun writing to the press to complain about hawking and Councillors have taken the issue up on behalf of their constituents.

The Minister is under pressure to initiate legislation on hawking to bring the trade under control in one way or another. To come up with a policy, he has appointed a **Special Committee on Hawking.** The Special Committee is made up of five Councillors from the legislature. Their brief is to come up with a policy document that can be used as a basis for developing legislation. The Committee is chaired by an ANC front-bencher called **Ms Gqubele,** and includes one NP front-bencher, one other ANC member, and two other less significant figures. **The Assistant Director for Inner-City Development** has been appointed by the **Director General, Dr Fanie Schoeman,** to act as a Secretariat for the Committee.

Dr Fanie Schoeman was a former Director-General in the old provincial administration and has managed to keep his position. In line with affirmative action policies, he has made one or two black appointments at a senior level. One of them is **Mr Malebo,** a trained development economist with a degree from an overseas university and a management diploma from a South African university. Dr Schoeman was tipped off informally that Mr Malebo was a member of the ANC – this counted in his favour when he applied for the job.

In order to develop a policy framework. Ms Gqubele has consulted all the stake-holders involved. She has been highly influenced by the RDP document, which points to the need to involve civil society in the development of policy, and has organised a one day workshop for all those involved. The aim is to discuss elements of the policy framework. She has worked closely with Mr Malebo to set up the workshop. Under pressure to deliver quickly due to increasingly violent tensions between hawkers and shop keepers, Gqubele wants a policy document soon.

> **HOW TO RUN THE ROLE PLAY:**
>
> Assign each team a briefing sheet and set a time period for participants to draw up a policy document which is acceptable to all parties concerned. The negotiations are to be chaired by Ms Gqubele. Each team is to negotiate within the constraints of the information provided to them on their briefing sheets. Whilst all teams are allowed to read the general information, the briefing sheets are confidential.

BRIEF FOR THE MINISTER:

You have a range of constituencies to consider:
- the unemployed who are forced into the informal sector;
- ordinary working people (both black and white) who walk on the pavements every day and complain about all the clutter and over-crowding;
- the shop owners who are well organised in a Shop Owners' Association some of whom are leading members of the ANC and therefore have political weight;
- the senior bureaucrats, many of whom argue that hawking impoverishes the city;
- the Hawkers' Association that is led by people who do not seem to be politically reliable;
- the Special Committee whose Chairperson is an ANC member, whom you know very well from the years of struggle.

You have been impressed by presentations made by the Technical Advisor of the Shop Owners' Association. The basic argument of the shop owners is as follows:
- hawking results from unemployment – to deal with it you need short and long-term solutions;
- hawking frightens off investors in the city and hence unemployment is made worse by hawking;
- it is necessary to bring hawking under control via an Act;
- the short term strategy should be to designate a specific area as a hawkers' market to which the hawkers should be relocated;
- by cleaning up the area from hawkers, investment will be attracted, jobs will be created and less people will be forced to resort to hawking.

Your Director-General likes this basic approach and has already begun to format the approach into a policy document that could be used as the basis for drafting legislation. However, he has agreed to participate in the consultations – but you know that he has already decided what should happen.

However, there are other voices that you need to listen to. At the end of the day, you must make the decision on what the policy should be.

BRIEF FOR MS GQUBELE, THE CHAIRPERSON OF THE COMMITTEE

This is your first major policy process. You want to learn from it, but also make an impact in what is a high-profile issue.

You have a close personal link with the Minister who you knew from the struggle days. He has made it clear that you must come up with something soon.

You also have quite a close link with members of the Executive of the Hawkers' Association – one of them used to be a shop steward in the Commercial Workers' Union in the 1980s when you were a union organiser. You are not very keen on the Chairperson, however. You suspect he is operating in a rather opportunist way.

You are worried about two members of your Committee. Your ANC colleague is quite a big shot in the ANC regional structure, but he was not really involved in the struggle in the 1980s. He has close links with the Chairperson of the Shop Owners' Association. You are also worried about the NP member who you suspect is on good terms with the Director General of the Department – a man that can sometimes influence the Minister.

Your main ally and support is Mr. Malebo. He seems to understand policy and the issues involved. He is efficient and gets things done. However, he seems a little naive at the political level.

You are aware that the shop owners are well organised and have developed technically competent proposals that have impressed the Minister. However, you need to find a way of resolving the problem without alienating the hawkers. After all, they are key voting members in your area and some are members of the ANC branch in one of the inner city areas where you live. You are not at all convinced that moving them into a hawkers' park will do the trick as has been proposed by the shop owners.

BRIEF FOR THE SHOP OWNERS AND BRUCE HANSON IN PARTICULAR:

You are a well organised constituency with a well funded association. Bruce Hanson is a capable and articulate Chairperson who is frequently on TV and in the press. He also recently joined the ANC in order to increase leverage on the Minister and to influence the Special Committee on Hawking.

Your position is straightforward: although you recognise that unemployment is what causes hawking, you want to end hawking as far as possible because it takes customers away from your shops and frightens off investment. Your main aim is to get the hawkers off the streets and into a special hawkers' market near the main station. This will cost money which you feel should come from the state.

With the support of the association and paid for by the association, you retained the services of an urban planner who was requested to devise a plan that will resolve the issue. This was done in the form of a very glossy-looking document that provided a very convincing case for how the inner cities could develop into major development nodes. However, the obstacle is the hawkers and therefore the planner recommended the concept of special hawkers' markets near the main stations. If this took place, the planner argued, then investment would be attracted back to the inner cities, employment would rise, less people would be forced into hawking and so, in the long run, the problem would be resolved.

One additional advantage that the planner brought into the situation is that he managed to develop quite a cosy relationship with the Chairperson of the Hawkers' Association, Mr Phaliso. Hanson is sure that the Minister will be finally convinced, particularly if the Chairperson of the Hawkers' Association supported the proposals. At a meeting with Mr Phaliso facilitated by the planner, Hanson proposed that the Shop Owners Association would sponsor a small business training programme to train hawkers to become formal business operators and that the association may even put up some venture capital to set up a small pilot group with a few shops of their own – a rather subtle way of offering Phaliso his own shop.

You are very worried about Ms Gqubele – she seemed rather hostile when you tried to lobby her. But at least you have one ally in the Special Committee who says he has the clout to out-manoeuvre Gqubele.

BRIEF FOR THE HAWKERS' ASSOCIATION:

As an association with quite a good membership, you have to deal with a strong groundswell of resistance against any changes to the existing unregulated situation. However, you are not well structured and you have no resources to rent offices or to hire the assistance of technical experts to help develop an alternative policy proposal to those that have been developed by the shop owners. All you can really do in the negotiations is to resist any proposal that suggests that you move. This is your bottom-line. However, you have problems.

It is clear that an increasing number of newly arrived hawkers are coming onto the streets. Some of these people are from foreign countries and are selling goods very cheaply. Others are coming from the rural areas and their stalls are dirty and badly run – this gives hawking a bad name. There is also an increase in crime and a number of women hawkers have been attacked and robbed. All these problems suggest that it is not really possible to simply demand that nothing is done and the existing situation is left to develop along its own lines.

The Executive is also divided. Mr Phaliso, the Chairperson, operates on his own and there is talk that he has been having individual meetings with Bruce Hanson. Others are quite close to Ms Gqubele, Chairperson of the Special Committee who seems sympathetic to the plight of the hawkers. Mr Malebo has been especially helpful. He has met some of the Executive members over weekends to help them develop ideas that go beyond the slogans. He suggested they find an NGO that can provide them with technical services. He made the point that all African cities have streets that are dominated by hawkers. The informal sector is here to stay and should actually be encouraged. This is how best to develop the economy. To think that investment in the inner city by businesses will create as many jobs as the informal sector is a dream. However, although the hawkers had ideas, they were never developed into a formal proposal.

BRIEF FOR THE DIRECTOR-GENERAL, DR FANIE SCHOEMAN:

You are quite familiar with the problem – you tried to deal with it in the Old South Africa and failed.

You like the ideas that have come from the shop owners. You are not convinced that getting rid of the hawkers from the streets will attract enough investment to reduce unemployment, but then, that is not the point of the exercise. The smelly, sweaty, clutter of those streets has destroyed the life and culture of the inner city areas – a life and culture that goes way back to the beginning of white civilisation in this area over a hundred years ago.

You are also a personal friend of the NP member of the Special Committee – you went to school together. The NP member also likes the proposals of the shop owners, but is very worried that by joining the ANC to get his proposals through to the Minister, Bruce Hanson will allow the ANC to get too much credit if the proposals are accepted. So the NP man has a dilemma – he is under pressure from the shop owners to support the proposals, but his party is worried that the ANC will get the credit.

You are sympathetic to your NP friend's political problem, but there is not much you can do about it at a political level. However, maybe you can do something about it at a technical level. As a result, you begin transforming the shop owners' proposals into a formal policy document with a problem statement, principles, options, etc. This is what you hope to give to the Minister as a way of supporting the shop owners. However, you have also decided to draft a Bill to translate the policy document into legislation. In discussions with the NP member of the Special Committee, you have shown him the Bill and suggested that maybe the NP can get credit by being the party that proposes the actual Bill. Professionally, however, you do not want to risk working directly for the NP man.

You have also met with Hanson, Phaliso and Gqubele – Gqubele worries you a lot because she seems to have a good link with the Minister. But in your discussions with the Minister, you think that he has seen the light and will go with the shop owners' proposals.

You have also hired Mr. Malebo and assigned him as Secretariat to the

Committee. In the final analysis, Malebo will have a lot of influence over what the Special Committee finally recommends.

BRIEF FOR THE ASSISTANT DIRECTOR:

You have been in the job for six months. Prior to that you were studying overseas and in South Africa.

The Director-General has assigned you as Secretariat to the Special Committee – this means that you have to work closely with Ms Gqubele who is someone you have admired over the years. You are also keen on this hawker's issue.

Your problem is that you know that the Director General favours the shop owners' proposals and that Schoeman often briefs the Minister without you being invited to the meetings. Because you have been working with Gqubele and the hawkers, you are more in favour of something that is in the interests of the hawkers. This links up to your Master's Thesis on the informal sector in African cities which found that the political economy of African cities is very dependent on the informal sector. Where governments have acted against the informal sector, poverty has increased and political instability has heightened. There are more creative ways of handling the problem, e.g. changing the structure of the streets; allocating corner shops to hawkers; designating certain streets for hawking; registering hawkers to limit uncontrolled expansion; numerous small markets, etcetera.

You have also had informal meetings with the hawkers to assist them.

THABISO MABONA AND THE LEEUWSTROOM HOUSING DEPARTMENT

Thabo Majoe and Lauren Blythe Schütte

Thabiso Mabona had recently accepted a position within the Housing Department of the Leeuwstroom local government. He was to be responsible for allocating housing for the approximately 2 300 people currently living in the informal settlement. His brief was very clear: he was to compile a list of families requiring housing within the following terms of reference: those families living in areas where there were no water or sewerage services were to receive priority, whilst families who earned over a certain amount were to provide houses for themselves. Discrimination, on any grounds, was not to be tolerated and a committee had been set up to monitor any irregularities. He was to report directly to the local management committee.

Initially, Thabiso felt he would be comfortable in this department. There were unambiguous reporting structures and the terms of reference seemed to offer very clear guidelines to help him draw up the lists. He looked forward to assisting the people of Leeuwstroom with their housing problems, particularly when he thought of the dwelling his parents had lived in when he was a boy.

After some time, it became clear to Thabiso that the job of drawing up the lists was not going to be as easy as he had originally thought. The guidelines were open to interpretation and the management committee had set in place a number of procedures which were making it extremely difficult for him to complete the task of allocating houses at the speed which the housing crisis required. The people currently occupying informal dwellings were getting extremely impatient and were threatening to occupy the newly-built houses if the allocation did not happen soon. Then, yesterday, out of the blue, he had been offered a way out of his difficulties by an old friend and he now found himself weighing up the costs and benefits of this offer.

BACKGROUND

Thabiso had come a long way from the dusty, crowded school on a farm near Leeuwstroom in the western Transvaal where he had lived with his grandmother as a child. Every day, until he had completed his schooling, he had walked the 10 kilometres to school, where he had shared a desk and school books with his best friend, Mpho. His parents had moved to an informal settlement outside

Leeuwstroom, which he visited occasionally, but it was considered safer for him to stay on the farm until he had completed his schooling.

By the time he was 27, Thabiso had not only graduated from one of the best institutions in the country but had also completed a diploma course at a university in Great Britain. On his return, he found a position as an officer in the Home Affairs Pension Department, which gave him responsibility for monitoring pension pay-out points. The position was not well paid and certainly not quite what he had hoped for, but he saw it as a stepping stone to greater things. After all, he had to start somewhere.

After a few months, Thabiso became aware that all was not right within the department. Organisationally things were a shambles. It seemed that dead people were receiving pensions and unaccompanied pensioners were being told that their pensions had been cancelled and were turned away empty-handed. Thabiso was genuinely concerned about the plight of the pensioners: he knew that in these times of high unemployment, whole families survived on the money brought in by pensioners, but he felt powerless to do anything about what was happening. Although his job description stipulated that he was to monitor pay-out points, it was unclear what he was to do when he discovered discrepancies. He had tried to bring up this matter with his immediate superior but he was brushed aside. This was serious, as his only means of access to higher authorities was through this superior.

He knew that there were others in the department who were unhappy with the situation but they seemed reluctant to do anything about it. He, too, was afraid of the consequences of blowing the whistle. He feared that he would lose his job. His parents were old and relied on his money at the end of the month so he couldn't afford to jeopardise his position. Although he had received a good education, he was young and inexperienced and he knew that jobs were scarce. Nevertheless, Thabiso felt uncomfortable about working in this department. He felt unable to carry out his job effectively and resolved to leave as soon as he could. In the meantime he would keep his head down and himself out of trouble.

MOVING TO THE LEEUWSTROOM HOUSING DEPARTMENT

Thabiso was pleased when the position at the Leeuwstroom Housing Department was offered to him. He felt that his career was finally going somewhere. As the weeks wore on, however, he became increasingly frustrated with the way things were working out. Again he felt that he was being prevented from doing his job properly, but this time it was not corruption that was the culprit but rigid procedures! The management committee had insisted that those applying for houses should provide substantial proof of their circumstances. This was making it practically impossible to draw up the lists. His desk was piled high with application forms. Everyone seemed to be in the same desperate situation but were rarely able to verify this. Where were people in informal settlements going to get documentation to prove their financial situation? He knew that pensioners were often paid cash without accompanying slips, and domestic workers were in the same position. Few people had bank accounts or any other documentation and he certainly did not have time to visit every dwelling to certify their claims. Thabiso felt that he was at a dead end!

THE OFFER

Last evening, Thabiso was alone in the office, just finishing up a few tasks before returning home when he heard the door open. He glanced up and saw a heavy-set man standing in the glare of the doorway. He squinted at the dark shadow and wondered who would be visiting the office at this time when everyone had gone home. "My friend, the office is closed. Come back tomorrow at 9 and someone will attend to you," he said.

The man walked further into the gloom of the office and, as he came closer, Thabiso shuddered with apprehension. The man leaned over the desk and the lamp shone on his face. After a few seconds, Thabiso's face broke into a broad grin. He stood up and slapped the man's outstretched hand. "Heh, heh, Mpho my old friend, good to see you after all these years. How are you?" Thabiso had heard that Mpho was operating a small law firm in the area and that he was part of the Leeuwstroom civic structure, but had not had the chance to reacquaint himself with his old friend. So many years had passed since they had seen each other last, and their experiences had been so different, that he had been unsure whether they would have anything to say to each other.

After a few minutes of catching up, talking of the old days in the dusty schoolyard, Mpho said "So, I hear you are responsible for drawing up the list for allocating new houses in the area. I hope you will be able to do the job better than the last person who was here! He was never able to draw up those lists."

They spoke a little about the allocation problems and how there had been a breakdown in relations between different sections of the community and the Housing Department. His predecessor had apparently alienated the civic movement by not consulting them on the process of allocation.

"I can make your life easier," said Mpho. "Let me help you draw up the list. I know what the interests of the community are and this way things will happen more speedily and everyone will be happy. You will not be sitting here hour after hour with a desk full of files. Let me suggest to you that the best way to draw up the list would be to place a public advertisement inviting applications from people who are seeking houses. All I ask is that you let me know when the advert is to be placed and let me have a pile of application forms beforehand. This will guarantee a speedy resolution to the matter and ensure that the right people get onto the list! If it would help I'm sure we can provide other incentives."

Thabiso watched his old friend disappear around the door. He felt depressed. He knew that a crisis was brewing and that if the houses were illegally occupied by angry people the council would have a serious problem on their hands. They would have no control over the collection of rents or anything else. Mpho's suggestion made sense: it would speed up the process and would possibly avert a crisis, but was it ethical? He could certainly put the idea of a public advert to the management committee – they seemed as flummoxed as he was about how to draw up the lists. But what about the matter of letting Mpho have the application forms before the public announcement? He did have legitimacy in the community, but was it fair? Thabiso wanted to see an end to this problem but wasn't sure whether Mpho's scheme was worth the risk. He picked up his jacket and headed for the door, wondering what he was to do.

CASE STUDY TWENTY-FOUR

AFFIRMATIVE ACTION IN THE ALEXANDRA/SANDTON TOWN COUNCIL

Haseena Rawat

> The central feature of affirmative action is that efforts are made on behalf of individuals because they belong to a particular racial or ethnic or cast communities. It is important to note that affirmative action is not intended to bridge the gap between the rich and poor but rather to bridge the gap between groups.
>
> *M Weiner, Professor of Political Science, Massachusetts Institute of Technology*

ADVERTISING FOR A COMMUNITY LIAISON CO-ORDINATOR

The Alexandra/Sandton Town Council had created a post for a Community Liaison Co-ordinator with a view to promoting peace and goodwill in surrounding communities and urgently needed to fill this position. The advert, placed in both the *Weekly Mail* and the *Sowetan*, required that prospective applicants possess a minimum degree in the social sciences with at least one year experience working in an NGO or a development oriented organisation. In addition, it was preferable if applicants were able to speak at least one African language. Mr Slabbert, Director of Human Resources in the council looked forward to filling the position with a suitable candidate in line with the Council's recently adopted Affirmative Action Policy. In terms of the policy, "the initial goal (was) skills representation per population group in the internal work-force, as reflected by the availability of such skills in the labour market".

THE CANDIDATES

Linda Gwala was the daughter of a high profile political activist, her parents left South Africa in 1960, to live in exile in the United Kingdom. Mr Gwala held a senior position in a popular mass movement in exile. Ms Gwala was born in London in 1965. On completion of her "A" Levels in London she went to Cuba where she completed a degree in Computer Science at the University of Cuba. She worked at the National Bank of London for two years in the capacity of a computer programmer. From 1992 onwards, she worked for Operation Hunger as a volunteer. In 1992 she returned to South Africa with her parents. She now lives with her parents in Dawn Park. She applied for the position advertised in the *Weekly Mail* and was called for an interview.

Pat Abrahams, a 29-year-old coloured woman, obtained a degree in sociology at the University of Western Cape. She worked for three years for the Department of Manpower in lieu of the bursary she received from the State to pursue her studies. In 1987, she moved to Johannesburg to work for an advice centre in Eldorado Park. She held executive positions in the Women's and Civic movements in the area. She shares a flat with friends in Eldorado Park. Like Ms Gwala she was short-listed to attend an interview for the advertised position at the Council.

Ms Gwala discussed her forthcoming interview with her best friend Zinzi. "I feel so anxious about my interview, I am not sure what is expected of interviews in this country. Furthermore I feel at a disadvantage not knowing what is supposed to be my mother tongue."

Ms Abrahams was looking forward to her interview, she was hopeful and optimistic due to her wide experience in NGOs. She saw the financial prospects that the job offered her as very appealing. "At least I can send more money home to my mother and son," she confided to her flat mate. "I know what it feels like to be poor as a child and do not want my son to experience the evils of poverty like myself." She oozed with confidence as she dressed for her interview. She looked forward to impressing the Council with her fluency in Xhosa which she learnt as a child growing up in Crossroads.

THE INTERVIEW

The date for the interviews arrived. Out of all the applications Ms Gwala and Ms Abrahams were short-listed. Mr Slabbert headed the panel of interviewers who made up the Multi-Cultural selection Committee of the Human Resource Department. Mr Slabbert wrote the following comments on the interview schedule in respect of the Ms Gwala:

> Ms Gwala is an intelligent woman with the following credentials: She has wide work experience in information technology; and some overseas experience in welfare work. She has a good command of the English language and looks forward enthusiastically to addressing the challenges facing South Africa. She meets with the requirements of the position.

On Ms Abrahams' interview schedule, he commented as follows:

> Ms Abrahams is an experienced articulate woman, who has been involved in NGOs and the developmental work for the past eight years. She has held responsible positions in organisations and feels confident that she can cope with the expectations of the position. She meets with the criteria necessary to fill the position.

After the interviews, Mr Slabbert thanked the women on behalf of the panel for their time; and reassured them that they would hear from him in the next two weeks.

THE VERDICT

Ten days later Ms Gwala received a memo by mail, congratulating her on her new appointment. She was pleased but nervous about being able to meet the demands of the position. She wondered whether she would cope adequately in a predominantly Zulu-speaking constituency.

On the same day, Ms Abrahams received a letter of regret. Although she had been a strong candidate, she had been unsuccessful in her application.

MANAGEMENT AT THE PEOPLE'S DEVELOPMENT CENTRE: A HARD NUT TO CRACK

Mpho Moeti

Ms Masondo, a well educated and highly articulate woman, works at the People's Development Centre (PDC) in Soweto. The mission of the Soweto PDC is to provide people within the community, particularly the unemployed youth in and around the township, with life skills. Ms Masondo feels that she has a real stake in the centre, as she was instrumental in setting it up. She is, however, frustrated by the inflexible management style of the organisation and is finding it more and more difficult to justify staying.

BACKGROUND

Ms Masondo previously worked as a junior officer on a similar project in Johannesburg, the Johannesburg Training Centre (JTC), which had been in existence for 15 years. For most of that time, the JTC had provided life skills training in the predominantly white communities in Johannesburg's poorer suburbs. However, with the changing demographics in these areas, the JTC management decided that the organisation needed to expand its client base and to employ black staff members to help them with this change.

Ms Masondo was one of the first black staff appointments to the JTC. She was a resident of Soweto and every day, as she made her way out of the township towards work, she was reminded of the need for such a project in her own backyard. "Who needs life skills training more than the youth in Soweto?" she asked herself. Pushed by her convictions, she had approached senior management with the idea and they had promptly put it forward to their donors. Everyone had agreed that a similar centre in Soweto was an excellent idea.

BUILDING SUPPORT

Ms Masondo conducted a comprehensive outreach programme, consulting widely amongst church groups; youth clubs; political organisations; community development agencies and social welfare agencies. She elicited enormous interest in the proposal and the subsequent pilot project proved so successful that the Soweto PDC soon got off the ground.

LEADERSHIP

When the PDC first opened, it was argued that there should be a transfer of management from the JTC until such time as Ms Masondo and other black officers had accumulated enough experience to be able to cope with the management of the centre themselves. Ms Masondo was unhappy about this decision as she felt that she was in a better position to understand the needs of the community than Mr Dysan, the Senior officer. She knew that he had been involved in a similar project for 15 years, but felt that he and his colleagues had a technical approach to people's needs which was inappropriate for the Soweto Centre. However, she accepted the situation knowing that she would soon prove that she was capable of running the centre.

She has argued consistently for black representation in the management structures of PDC, but with no success.

Ms Masondo, being a Soweto resident, has her ear to the ground and knows that there is a growing feeling amongst the beneficiaries that, although the project is beneficial, it is not directly responsive to their specific needs. Repeated failures to make management respond to this problem has left Ms Masondo feeling frustrated. She feels that despite other promising signs of long-term sustainability of the project, such as stable funding and community support, the inflexible management style has the potential to destroy the project. She feels that she cannot continue working under these conditions and contemplates leaving the project since Mr Dysan and his colleagues are such hard nuts to crack. She cannot see how to convince them that their management style could have negative consequences for the project.

CASE STUDY TWENTY-SIX

PETER MAHLANGU AND THE DEPARTMENT OF PUBLIC WORKS

Samson Baloyi

Mr Peter Mahlangu's rise to the position of head of the Civil Engineering Section in the Department of Public Works in Region G of the Federal State of South Africa had not come as any surprise. He was, after all, a very talented young man of 29 and much was expected of him.

Peter obtained his engineering degree at the University of Cape Town with flying colours and duly fulfilled the requirements of the Association of South African Engineers for registration as a professional engineer. Throughout his studies, he had been sponsored by the government's public service commission bursary and indeed it was felt to be a worthwhile investment since it was anticipated that he would come back to serve the public. Peter was a deeply religious person. For him, serving disadvantaged people was the highest priority. He vowed that he would use his newly-won position to develop his people in whatever way possible.

His appointment as head of the Civil Engineering Section came about after he had worked in the department for three years. The position had previously been held by Mr Hans Kriel, who had just retired, for ten years. It was generally felt that he had not run the section efficiently and effectively. He had lacked the required qualifications and, indeed, there had been many problems during his tenure. His retirement had provided the department with the ideal opportunity to promote a black professional into the higher ranks in the department.

As head of a section, Peter's tasks included participation in the tender-board, which was a subsection of the Finance Department. He was also a member of both the departmental committee responsible for submitting recommendations for the appointment of project contractor and the committee that made recommendations on the appointment of consultants for civil projects.

In the past few years there had been a mushrooming of black civil contractors and the number of tenders the department had received from this sector had increased dramatically. Black contractors, however, had had little success in winning contracts from the public sector, and contracts continued to be awarded primarily to white contractors. Black contractors admitted that they lacked experience and skills in the tendering process, but knew that during Mr Kriel's reign as head of the section, they had not been given a fair chance. They had high hopes that Peter's appointment would greatly improve their chances.

Many black contractors approached Peter individually and collectively to ask for his assistance and advice in the tendering process. Peter acknowledged the problems they were facing and saw the need to address them. He knew that he had the skill to assist but felt that due to his heavy workload, the only way he could do so was outside of his working hours. As a member of the Association of South African Engineers, however, Peter had to operate under their code of ethics which, amongst other things, does not allow a registered professional who is employed by the public sector to operate a private consultancy. This prevented him from helping those who came to him for assistance. Peter realised that the black contractors needed him as much in the department as outside of it, but he could not be in both places at the same time.

Peter was soon faced with another dilemma. As a member of the tender board, he was prevented from divulging details of tender documents, particularly those regarding budgets, to contenders. Secrecy prevented the ultimate bidding price of the project from being influenced. He had, however, been approached by a group of black contractors who had proposed that he disclose tendered budgets to them to increase their chances of being awarded contracts. They argued that when Mr Kriel had been in his position white contractors had been privy to this information as a matter of course. Peter did not know what to do. He knew the code of ethics of the tender board had been undermined by Mr Kriel, and that by following his example he would be able to redress the imbalances of the past, but his conscience told him that this was not the right thing to do.

Before long Peter began to receive gifts from consulting firms which had traditionally been appointed for projects in public works. Concerned, he approached his seniors regarding the policy on receiving gifts and was told that under no circumstances was he to accept them. However, he saw gifts being given to senior officials and no-one seemed to notice. When he rejected a gift that was offered to him the surprised consultant told him that senior officials within the department had been accepting gifts for as long as he could remember and that this was the first time anyone had turned down a gift.

Peter felt concerned. Not only was he having to adjust to the responsibilities and workload which came with his new position, but every day his integrity was being tested. He seemed to have two options: either to ignore the ethics codes which governed his position and his profession, thereby helping himself and those black consultants who were battling to be awarded contracts, or to stand by his principles and do what he considered to be the right thing.

CASE STUDY TWENTY-SEVEN

CRACKING THE CULTURE CODE: THE WAY INTO THE INNER CIRCLE

T J Mokou

One Monday morning, two weeks after he had joined Spoornet as an Affirmative Action Officer, Lehurutshe Ngutshane entered his office and found a brown envelope lying on his desk. Inside he found two tickets to the Wanderers Club Golf Tournament for the next Saturday. He wondered who could have invited him to such a prestigious event. It wasn't quite the Sun International Million Dollar Challenge but he knew that it was considered something of an occasion.

When his secretary Diana came back to the office after her usual tea-time chat with her friends, he asked who had brought the envelope to his office. "It was personally delivered by Mr Scott." she told him. "Hmm, hand-delivered by the General Manager," thought Lehurutshe as he returned to his office.

To be honest, Lehurutshe found golf rather tedious. He never watched it on TV and most certainly had never played it. He was a soccer man himself. Somehow he could not see himself giving up his usual weekend activities and making the trip back into town from Soweto for the golf tournament on Saturday. Besides, he had a date that evening.

Lehurutshe rang the event organiser and excused himself from the tournament, saying he would be attending a neighbour's funeral on that day. "What a pity," he was told, "this really is a good opportunity for you to get to know Mr Scott and the MD."

At the golf tournament, Lehurutshe's absence was noticed. The MD asked questions about him. The GM asked questions about him. They were told he had gone to a funeral. "Typical! Just like my maid! " muttered the MD under his breath. "These events are important; this is the only time people get to understand each other."

On Monday morning, Lehurutshe noticed a slight chill in the atmosphere at work. People were bustling around, chatting about the tournament. The MD walked straight past him. The GM walked straight past him. A colleague asked him how the funeral was. "What funeral?" asked Lehurutshe. "I heard the MD saying you had gone to a funeral." "Well I did but I did not tell him I was going."

He wondered how everyone knew he had gone to a funeral. He called Diana into his office. "Tell me, Diana, how come everyone is so excited by the golf tournament – do you guys get a bonus for going or what?"

"One thing you will have to learn about working here is that it is important to be in the right place at the right time," said Diana. "Your next chance will be the J&B in Durban – miss two occasions and you've blown it. Everyone will begin to question your loyalty to the company."

From that time on, Lehurutshe felt alienated. He felt that he was being watched and that people were suspicious of him. Having to go out with the bosses was not something he had anticipated in his career. He did a full day's work, often staying late if work was incomplete. Weekends were his own time, for being with his family and friends in Soweto.

Lehurutshe didn't last more than three months with the company. He knew he had blown it, so he resigned. His successor, Robert Moremi, lived in Bramley and had been a trainee manager with Spoornet for two years. Lehurutshe had agreed to induct Robert into the job before he left. A few days later the MD personally delivered an invitation to Robert for the J&B in Durban the following weekend. "Fantastic!" said Robert. "I'll be there!" Robert would fit well into the inner circle at Spoornet, Lehurutshe thought bitterly, whereas he simply had not managed to crack the code in time.

CASE STUDY TWENTY-EIGHT

MOUNTAIN RIDGE WORKING GROUP: A NEW RESPONSE TO INNER CITY CHALLENGES

Lorelle Menné and Mark Bear

INTRODUCTION

Mountain Ridge is a suburb close to the Central Business District, so close that it is seen as an integral part of the urban core. It is a district which has a rich and chequered history and, in its present incarnation, captures all that is both vibrant and tawdry in the new South Africa. As the cumbersome laws limiting where people could live disintegrated, inner city areas exerted a mesmerising influence both on those who had, and those who sought, work in the CBD. Mountain Ridge was no exception. Lying on a ridge overlooking the city, the area is dense with apartment buildings which provide a large number of housing units for eager tenants. The combination of the pull of the city and access to accommodation has led to Mountain Ridge very quickly becoming the most populous borough, *pro rata*, in any metropolitan area in the country. Sadly, the quality of the housing and the vast increase in population has resulted in Mountain Ridge gaining the reputation, with some justification, of a "problem" area. This relates not just to overcrowding, but increasingly to crime, service provision and a range of other issues.

THE ROLE OF THE CITY COUNCIL

In mid-January 1992 the Management Committee of the City Council decided to address the degeneration of Mountain Ridge. Accordingly, the Council put forward a proposal to establish a working group, with Councillor Maroody, Head of Housing and Urbanisation and member of the Management Committee, as Chairperson.

The Council, as Convenor, invited representatives of a range of community and service organisations, such as resident associations, trader associations and the local police. One of the attendees was Devi Naidoo, a product of the civic organisations of the 1980s, and more recently a member of the Urbanisation Department.

FORMATION OF THE MOUNTAIN RIDGE WORKING GROUP

The outcome of this proposal was the establishment of the Mountain Ridge Working Group (MRWG) in February 1995. The Group's first task was to tackle the problem of littering in Mountain Ridge and to launch a campaign to create a more positive attitude towards the cleanliness of the area. Devi was appointed to serve on the MRWG. Meetings occurred on a regular basis over a period of several months. It was during this time that the Council, seeking further support from within its own ranks, drafted Cyril du Toit into the Group. Cyril had worked as a research manager for 10 years, first in a literacy NGO and later as Director of the Centre for Local Government Studies. He moved across to the Council in November 1994 and soon after was promoted to Director of the Urbanisation Department.

RESTRUCTURING

The lack of resources available to the Group was a consistent problem and, for this reason, among others, little of substance emerged from their meetings apart from a couple of minor anti-litter initiatives. At around the same time that it became clear that some form of restructuring was necessary, the Student Affairs Department at the nearby university approached the MRWG with a strong proposal that the whole approach to the issue of crime in Mountain Ridge be reviewed. While the police felt that an adequate job was being done in terms of policing the area, local community organisations disagreed. A workshop was held, involving representatives of the MRWG and interested community and service organisations, including representatives of Council.

The effect of this workshop was to outline a *modus operandi* for the MRWG as a whole. "It was a very fortunate coincidence that this issue – a grassroots problem – emerged when it did," says Devi. "It transformed our thinking at a crucial point in the Group's development." As a result, a subcommittee was formed, driven by the Urbanisation Department, to formulate and co-ordinate a proposal for the restructuring of the MRWG. The department held a series of meetings with interested MRWG stakeholders. From these discussions, in addition to those held separately by the MRWG, a more ambitious version of the MRWG was tabled. It was no longer just a neighbourhood clean-up initiative but sought to deal with the broader physical, social and other problems in Mountain Ridge. "The consensus," Devi notes, "was that, first, the approach needed to be issue-based and, second, that there had to be community involvement, in other words, that the MRWG needed to appeal on a stakeholder basis." As a result, the role of the MRWG changed to one of co-ordination, liaison and strategy.

TASK TEAMS

Four task teams were set up to tackle key problems, namely:
- housing
- crime, safety and security
- community services and facilities
- economic advancement and marketing

The Urbanisation Department, for its part, tried to consolidate this expansion by making officials from the department available to help the task teams to meet, to strategise, and to try to bind the process and take it forward.

This task group approach constituted a breakthrough in Council thinking in terms of its developmental emphasis. However, the approach was in keeping with other initiatives in which Council participated, such as the Greater Metropolitan Council and the Central City Partnership (comprising Council, the community and the private sector).

The Traditional Approach

How would this kind of issue have been handled traditionally? The Council's traditional role is to provide services and to regulate them. Given that the problem was tackling littering, the Council's *modus operandi* would have been to arrange for personnel to clear up the litter, to police the area and issue offenders with fines. Even if a department such as Solid Waste had been charged with initiating a campaign to address the problem, public involvement would have been very limited. Equally, the internal process would have followed strictly functional lines: there would have been no integration between departments.

The Task Team Approach

How did the task group differ in approach? The Economic Advancement and Marketing Group, for example, sought to address the issue of informal traders in the area. As the population of the area had grown so had its needs. Thus the streets were filled with traders of all kinds – offering fruit and vegetables, jewellery, T-shirts, shoe repairs. It was a thriving and energetic marketplace, but the haphazard mushrooming of these stands has resulted in crowded pavements and congested streets and in the creation of new stakeholders in the Mountain Ridge network.

It was to define, and engage with, this new group of stakeholders that the Economic Advancement and marketing Group conducted extensive research into the needs of informal traders and their role in the new Mountain Ridge, as it was felt that their views should be incorporated into a broader economic strategy. After completing an in-depth survey, the task group returned in April 1995 and put forward the following recommendations:

- that the Council establish a market for the informal traders;
- that the market be established on Council property on Ewald Street;
- that further land on Ridge Street be used for parking;
- that pedestrian malls be considered as a matter of urgency on prime shopping streets, to include an informal component;
- that a code of conduct be agreed between informal and formal traders and the City Council.

In addition to these specific recommendations, the task group put forward a broader view of how the MRWG should involve all traders and, in fact, all residents, so that the community should have a part in defining a vision for Mountain Ridge and the role its economic component should play in that vision.

The Council was very keen to foster this sense of engagement. Cyril expresses the view: "We need to increase participation and move away from the communitie's perception of a Council initiative to a Council-initiated project, which has its own dynamic. The Council can make space for things to happen, but residents and traders have to take the opportunity to make things happen themselves. The underlying approach is to develop a vision of urban development as something not just brought about by the City Council, but that Council resources, and those from elsewhere in the community, are brought together so that a synergy is developed. While large cities need integrated planning for transport and other forms of infrastructure, they are too big to be regarded as a unified community. So the initiatives of the MRWG serve as a means of developing that sense of community and shared values."

COUNCIL AS A DEVELOPMENT PARTNER?

As the Council strives to gain credibility, it is faced with a new question: legitimacy of its initiative. In other words, what happens when local government ceases to be just a service provider and regulator, and engages with active organisations in the neighbourhood? Development implies entrepreneurial activity, and it is not easy for the Council to be entrepreneurial – for good reason. Cyril feels that this poses a real threat: "If Council is a development partner with a set of Mountain Ridge residents, then you might say that those who have participated in MRWG now have a special status with the Council, in that we are working specifically with them as a particular set of interest groups to achieve particular goals in Mountain Ridge." Becoming involved with specific players could break down the barrier of rules governing how public servants deal with the public. It also, in a worst case scenario, opens up opportunities for special deals, for 'crony'-ism.

Furthermore, it raises the question of deployment of Council money and resources. In principle, the function of bureaucracy is to define a set of rules that ensures that public money is deployed in an equitable way. Should the Council put more into, say, Mountain Ridge, given that people in this neighbourhood are better organised than in another? While this would convey the message that Council rewards an entrepreneurial spirit and affirms the value of organisation, what of the communities which are not organised but more needy?

If the Council is justified in not making its resources quite so readily available to the MRWG, how would the MRWG be funded? Cyril has no doubt: "I would like to see the group generate resources, not just from the Council, but more broadly, from other constituents in Mountain Ridge, such as the private sector and development agencies. There is no reason why they should not put money into something which can demonstrate that it has its own kind of momentum. The key is that the MRWG must come up with its own set of projects. At the moment it is still a set of discussions. That's fine, but at some point it has to start delivering."

QUESTIONS FOR DISCUSSION:

1. Has Cyril du Toit defined appropriately the problem facing civil servants who seek to promote participatory development?
2. What strategies are available to him to resolve the problem?
3. What should his advice to Devi be on how to manage the MRWG in future?

INDEX

CASE STUDIES KEYED TO TOPICS

Development Management
Cases: 1; 6; 11; 22; 23; 26; 28

Education Management
Cases: 4; 5; 9

Ethics
Cases: 1; 10; 11; 12; 13; 17; 19; 23; 26

Finance and Economics
Cases: 1; 11; 26

Health Management
Cases: 16

Human Resources Management
Cases: 2; 4; 5; 7; 8; 9; 10; 16; 18; 24; 25; 27

Local Government
Cases: 6; 15; 17; 22; 23; 28

Management of Diversity
Cases: 1; 10; 24; 27

Management of Change
Cases: 1; 2; 3; 4; 5; 7; 13; 14; 20

Organisational Theory
Cases: 2; 7; 8; 9; 14; 17; 18; 20; 25; 27

Police
Cases: 20

Policy
Cases: 6; 15; 21

Role of the State
Cases: 2; 3; 6; 19; 28

Strategy
Cases: 3; 4; 5; 6; 7; 14; 16; 19; 22; 28